UNIVERSITY OF NORTH CAROLINA AT CHAPEL HILL
DEPARTMENT OF ROMANCE LANGUAGES

NORTH CAROLINA STUDIES
IN THE ROMANCE LANGUAGES AND LITERATURES

Founder: URBAN TIGNER HOLMES
Editor: CAROL L. SHERMAN

Distributed by:

UNIVERSITY OF NORTH CAROLINA PRESS

CHAPEL HILL
North Carolina 27515-2288
U.S.A.

NORTH CAROLINA STUDIES IN THE
ROMANCE LANGUAGES AND LITERATURES
Number 277

AN EARLY BOURGEOIS LITERATURE IN GOLDEN AGE SPAIN

LAZARILLO DE TORMES, GUZMÁN DE ALFARACHE
AND BALTASAR GRACIÁN

AN EARLY BOURGEOIS LITERATURE IN GOLDEN AGE SPAIN

LAZARILLO DE TORMES, GUZMÁN DE ALFARACHE AND BALTASAR GRACIÁN

BY
FRANCISCO J. SÁNCHEZ

CHAPEL HILL

NORTH CAROLINA STUDIES IN THE ROMANCE
LANGUAGES AND LITERATURES
U.N.C. DEPARTMENT OF ROMANCE LANGUAGES

2003

Library of Congress Cataloging-in-Publication Data

Sánchez, Francisco J., 1959-
  An early bourgeois literature in golden age Spain: Lazarillo de Tormes, Guzmán de Alfarache and Baltasar Gracián / by Francisco J. Sánchez.
   p. cm. – (North Carolina Studies in the Romance Languages and Literatures; no. 277).
   Includes bibliographical references.
   ISBN 0-8078-9280-7 (pbk.)
   1. Spanish prose literature–Classical period, 1500-1700–History and criticism. 2. Middle class in literature. 3. Lazarillo de Tormes. 4. Alemán, Mateo, 1547-1614? Aventuras y vida de Guzmán de Alfarache. 5. Gracián y Morales, Baltasar, 1601-1658–Criticism and interpretation. I. Title. II. Series.

PQ6249.A5S26 2003
868'.30809355–dc21   2003054125

Cover design: Heidi Perov

© 2003. Department of Romance Languages. The University of North Carolina at Chapel Hill.

ISBN 0-8078-9280-7

DEPÓSITO LEGAL: V. 5.416 - 2003

ARTES GRÁFICAS SOLER, S. L. - LA OLIVERETA, 28 - 46018 VALENCIA

TABLE OF CONTENTS

	Page
PREFACE	11
CHAPTER 1: THE WEALTH AND THE LITERATURE OF THE *REPÚBLICA*	15
CHAPTER 2: A BOURGEOIS SELF. THE CHRISTIAN PERSON IN THE WORLD	70
CHAPTER 3: A LITERARY SOCIETY WITHIN THE SEIGNIORIAL SOCIETY. CULTURE AND LIFE IN GRACIÁN	99
CHAPTER 4: A MERCANTILE CONSCIOUSNESS. *GUZMÁN DE ALFARACHE* AND GRACIÁN ON WEALTH	123
CONCLUSION	151
BIBLIOGRAPHY	153

ACKNOWLEDGMENTS

I want to express my gratitude to the University of Iowa Office of the Vice President for Research that funded my project with an Arts and Humanities Initiative award, and to the Office of the Provost that provided a Research Assignment that allowed me to dedicate full time to the completion of the manuscript; and again to the Office of the Vice President for Research, the College of Liberal Arts and Sciences, and the Department of Spanish and Portuguese of the University of Iowa for their generous support in the publication of this book.

I am grateful to Jennifer Cooley for sharing with me her time and refined talents doing a throughout editing of the first draft of the manuscript. I received very valuable suggestions also from Helen Ryan while writing a section of the first chapter. Although the translation of quotes from Spanish texts is entirely my responsibility, credit is due to Luis Marxuach who helped me with some quotes for a section of the first chapter.

A section of chapter 1 was published with the title "A Discourse on Wealth in Golden Age Literature" in the volume *Culture and the State in Spain: 1550-1850*, London: Garland Press, 1999. 55-101.

PREFACE

THIS book proposes to read the picaresque novels *Lazarillo de Tormes* (1554) and Mateo Alemán's *Guzmán de Alfarache* (1599, 1604), and the texts of Baltasar Gracián (1601-1658) as the major representatives of an early bourgeois literature in Golden Age Spain.

The study assumes the argument in current historiography that Early Modern Spain arises along the tensions between a seigniorial power and an emergent bourgeois society. Along this background, I argue that from about 1555 to about 1630 we can detect an early conceptualization of a sphere of economic exchanges differentiated from the values of the rentier classes behind the Habsburg's dynasty and the Church. As the space for the circulation of wealth, the *república* configures the economic grounding for an emergent bourgeois sensibility that would influence the literary representation of major moral and religious issues.

Furthermore, I investigate the notions of the "person," "culture" and "life" in these texts. My argument benefits from theoretical analyses regarding the formation of a private sphere of social action and the formation of a literary sphere to represent early bourgeois values and feelings, what I shall call the "literature of the *república*." Within Thomist philosophy the "person" was a term used to define a human being as an "individual" whom God has endowed with reason, free will and self-determination. I discern, however, evidence of a major social change in the novel *Lazarillo de Tormes*. With the expression "my person," this text starts to represent a space of privacy. Expanding J. C. Rodríguez's analysis of a bourgeois ideology in Lázaro's narration of "his own life," I argue that also Lázaro's person belongs to his own life, in distinction to any other life of any other person. His person is the attribute that the *yo* (the I) discloses in his narration, not merely in relation to other "individual entities" but among other persons. Lázaro's person is on his way to individuality and self-consciousness and, while these more contemporary terms will acquire full expression with the outcome of a full bourgeois society, they configure the horizon of a secular self-determination. In the novel *Guzmán de Alfarache* Mateo Alemán grants his *pícaro* with even more self-confidence in terms of the economic possibilities of the person. The *pícaro* is often engaged in a transaction and his person socially grows by responding to economic needs and by his drive for enrichment.

Years later, the notion of the person in Baltasar Gracián signals yet another change in the Christian idea. I argue that Gracián emphasizes the attribute of self-determination and, as in *Lazarillo*, the person becomes the term used to discriminate among human beings rather than among individual entities in the theological sense. Moreover, Gracián describes the person as a goal attained by select individuals who reach a higher degree of cultural differentiation from the *vulgo* (populace) and the *gentes* (people).

In Gracián's view, the attainment of success requires the development of a private "reason of state." The person's success becomes an emblem of his intellectual and moral attributes. By his own "reason of state," he acquires a civil sovereignty, a symbolic and intellectual power through which he navigates the spheres of individualized confrontation in search for benefits or wealth.

I make use of Habermas's concept of a "literary sphere" in early modernity to argue that, for Gracián, "culture' is the self-understanding that the person has of a literary society. The person sees his belonging to this society as a value that transcends both, the restrictions imposed on him within the "society of the court," and the incivility perceived in the rest of the world.

This early literary society elaborates on the symbolic values of the *república*, such as the "refined conversation" among citizens praised by Humanist writers. Gracián situates culture within an intellectual life of select individuals and in the context of a new political morality. The intimate relationship between writing and culture and between these two terms and the social process of "life" declares the exclusively intellectual understanding that Gracián has of the person.

However, it is this intellectual outlook what allows him to elaborate on the verbal, rhetorical and literary aspects of social dealings.

In this sense, the literary world represents the transition from the restrictions that the seigniorial society imposes on "life" and individual development, to the self-assertion and personal growth that the bourgeois society promotes.

My analysis of intellectual wealth benefits from the notion of "symbolic capital" elaborated by Bourdieu. I intend to show that picaresque literature portrays the way social actors conceive an economic dimension in the cultural values of the seigniorial society. Moreover, intellectual and verbal skills become, in Gracián's outlook, instruments of the person to advance strategically within an emergent world defined by a growing competition.

The person seems to perceive that human exchanges are conducted intentionally to confuse and defeat him. Furthermore, this intentional conduct configures a field of "appearances" where Gracián observes, in my view, the disintegration of substantial notions of the "world." Moreover, appearances become symbolic goods of a social capital that the person advances in order to obtain a profit over the rest of competitors by interpreting their verbal deceptions.

Appearances are, then, the product of skillful persons that seek to increase their social value. In this sense, appearances show the degree of sovereignty and the extent of the person's intellectual wealth. They are cultural signs of the level of confrontation, and their ambiguity infuses a high degree of suspicion and insecurity in all the actors, transforming social transactions in micro-battles where the whole person is at stake.

The *pícaro* and Gracián's hero partake, then, of a similar secularized sensibility. They portray a process of individuation tainted by a fundamental distrust in any inter-personal contact. In this sense, an appeal to God seems to support either a mercantile consciousness –in the case of the *pícaro* Guzmán– or a spirituality ostensibly at odds with the conflictive fight for success –in the case of Gracián's hero.

The world of appearances is prominently a verbal space in which the intentional conduct of people presents an analogy with a self-conscious use of language. In Gracián, this intellectual convergence between social and literary worlds reinforces the notion of the person as the outcome of an increasing sophistication of language and, thus, as the product of the cultural exchanges taking place in a new civil society.

CHAPTER 1

THE WEALTH AND THE LITERATURE OF THE *REPÚBLICA*

AN EARLY *REPÚBLICA*

> la ley obliga a los ciudadanos no de otro modo que un cierto contrato, por eso la ley se llama y lo es en realidad, una especie de contrato. (Vázquez de Menchaca III, 41)
>
> (In no other way but as a kind of contract the law obliges the citizens; so it is that the law is called, and truly is, a type of contract.)

THE bourgeois state will be founded on the principle of the contract. In general terms a contract is the free engagement of people in a promise that may result in benefit or loss, but that in any case is a promise that binds them. To reach that point, the bourgeoisie had to radically transform the old notion of natural law in order to substantially rethink the ideas about domination and, forced by historical circumstances, even the concepts that addressed a progressively broader international politics.

By 1554 Spain had become an Empire. The legitimization of the domination of the Indians was not, however, a simple matter to be dealt with by recourse to the Holy-Roman Imperial ideology. What right had Spain that England or France did not have? The whole American continent was outside the ancient Roman boundaries, thus making unlikely the acceptance by any other European Kingdom the Habsburg's fanciful claim to possess a privilege in the new territories based on historical rights.

The Bulls granted by Pope Alexander VI in 1493 became a matter of conflict because all other European powers rejected the Imperial ambitions of both the Church and the Castilian kingdom. They saw in the Papal concession a threat to a balanced relation of force across the continent, particularly at the time when the universal influence of the Catholic Church was being dismantled. The disagreement over the Spanish claims generated political controversies that would last well into the next century forcing military and diplomatic scenarios where each actor intended to benefit from a changing geo-political structure.

The American colonization turned out to be a crucial factor in the development of a merchant capital, especially in terms of reserve funds that the investment on the extraction and commercialization of gold and silver helped to accumulate at the banks and national Treasuries. In addition, the dynamics of an aggression as the instrument that better suited the defensive needs of each kingdom accelerated the intellectual innovation of many sectors of the learned people. Describing these polemics, Pagden has underscored the importance of the internal intellectual dissension, that is the opposition that the Imperial thrust encountered in some Spanish theologians:

> The arguments directed against the Bulls by the English and the French depended upon a denial of the Papacy's implicit assumption of jurisdiction in both the spiritual and the temporal sphere, and of Alexander's still more contentious claim to exercise *dominium* over both Christians and pagans [. . .]
>
> The neo-Thomist theologians and civil lawyers (though not, unsurprisingly, the canonists) who worked at Salamanca in the sixteenth century –the so-called 'School of Salamanca'– rejected the authority of the Bulls on precisely the same grounds. The Pope was, they recognized, the spiritual ruler of all Christians. But he could exercise no *dominium* in the secular world, nor had he authority of any kind over non-Christians. (Pagden 47)

Many Spanish writers perceived in the Imperial drive a serious obstacle for the development of a strong Spanish Monarchy that could compete for the European supremacy, while promoting the creation of wealth in Castile. To guarantee the security of Spanish borders the Monarchy would have to free itself from the drive of a universal domination. Political writers developed strong interpretations of natural law theory in order to justify or to oppose the colonization of the Indies.

In any case, they understood that a growing European inter-relationship involved the demise of a straightforward hegemony of a single nation because an overextended territorial power could jeopardize the possibilities of the growth of each kingdom. At the same time, the development of a modern international law took for granted the interests of an emergent merchant State, since natural law –they thought– established the natural right of people to move freely and exchange goods for the survival of all nations. Restrictions and violent opposition to this freedom was a legitimate cause of war. This legitimacy could have full force only if military and territorial imperialism was compensated by the development of a national civil society.

No nation could, in principle, claim any universal authority. There was no essential domination of one nation over the other. Political authority was the result of the pursuit of the people's welfare, and in this sense authority was a "right" of the people to live peacefully. No theory of domination could be established before the concrete power relations, and no hierarchy of forces could be developed in the abstract but out of the actual positions of nations.

The conjuncture created by the mutual limitations among kingdoms exacerbated the tenor of the political debate. It had as a consequence the translation of the concept of free will to the realm of politics, that is the conceptualization of an "acceptance" on the part of the subject. Out of the debates on the limits and hierarchy among nations, Vázquez de Menchaca could not avoid putting forward a theory of political freedom. It is in the realm of "nations" where he seems to theorize the State as a contract on power:

> La autoridad es también de derecho natural; porque se dice pertenecer al derecho de gentes, lo que la mayor parte de los pueblos observan y admiten en la práctica ante las exigencias y necesidades humanas [. . .] como este derecho ya sea natural o de gentes, no lleve consigo una absoluta necesidad, sino solo causativa, a saber, para pasar la vida de un modo más conveniente, síguese, que nadie puede ser obligado contra su voluntad y oposición a vivir bajo la autoridad de otro. (Vázquez de Menchaca II, 52-3)

> (Authority belongs also to natural law; because it belongs to common law which is observed and practiced by most of the people to deal with human needs [. . .] since this law, either nat-

ural or common, does not carry an absolute necessity, but only a derivative, which means that is directed to have a more convenient life, it follows that nobody against his will can be forced to live under somebody else's authority.)

Eventually, the space of freedom outside an absolute or essential domination will be the civil society. The contract that people like Vázquez de Menchaca and Francisco Suárez had in mind was the base of an "artificial" or positive society which would conflate later on with the political society, the structure of the diverse functions of the State. Moreover, the freedom between nations and the relation between authority and its subjects correspond to the subordination of power to the principle of the contract, that is to the principle that individuals, as well as nations, engage in dealings with each other out of their own interests:

> el mero príncipe no es superior sino inferior a las leyes [. . .] la violación de las leyes por el príncipe debe considerarse como un acto perjudicial a la república. (Vázquez de Menchaca I 298)
>
> (the prince himself is not superior but inferior to the law [. . .] violation of laws by the prince must be considered a harmful act to the republic.)

The *república* is the domain of growth and welfare. The *república* is what theologians, economists and political economists (*arbitristas*) discuss when they argue about the political and moral implications of the state of the economy. It is a social sphere that emerges in distinction to the authority of the king and the *dominium* the Monarchy exercises over its kingdoms.

Following natural law doctrine, Suárez insists that the source of political power lies in the social body and exists in the community. However, there is nothing in natural law to determine the concrete arrangements to enforce this power, leaving the matter to positive law, that is to the historical developments of political forms:

> by the nature of things, men as individuals possess to a partial extent (so to speak) the faculty for establishing, or creating, a perfect community; and, by virtue of the very fact that they establish it, the power in question does come to exist in this community as a whole. Nevertheless, natural law does not require either that

> the power should be exercised directly by the agency of the whole community, or that it should always continue to reside therein. (Suárez 383)

Since there is no essential political form –natural law talks only negatively on this issue– political subjection can be articulated according to historical factors and the needs of the society.[1] Moreover, the legal order is the order that society imposes on itself to aspire to a better state. Suárez also sees in the legal order the means to enforce a moral duty by which society accepts being governed:

> For Law is (so to speak) an instrument by means of which the prince exercises a moral influence upon the state, in order that he may govern it. (Suárez 93)

Furthermore, the close identification between authority and society's objectives permits a "personalization" of power, that is a political reconsideration of the notion of *persona*. The welfare of society is embodied in the "prince," in the individual with power who becomes, in turn, a "public" belonging; or rather, he becomes the "public" dimension of persons:

> in the first place, the welfare of the prince, viewed as such, is considered as the common welfare, inasmuch as he is a public personage [*persona* in the original Latin] pertaining to the whole community. (Suárez 97)

Over and above the theatrical –Ancient– meaning, Christian philosophy had installed the person in the sphere of the self-determined being, the indivisible conjunction between material individuality and spiritual participation in God. By its spiritual projection, the person was supposed to acquire the level of autonomy and self-determination with which he could act according to reason and out of his free will.

With a transposition to political theory, Suárez seems to connote here a trajectory that a few years later another Jesuit writer –Baltasar Gracián– will follow with the term "persona." This trajectory establishes the person as the subject of a political morality in-

---

[1] "Monarchy is the best government only because it is a customary form," writes Suárez (p. 383).

sofar the person is the one who qualifies to reach a social sovereignty. Gracián will even consider the person to belong to the sphere of cultural distinction and, particularly, to the field of literature where the person may meet its peers.[2]

Suárez's "public person" emerges many years before Hobbes's "artificial person," that is the person with political sovereignty that exercises power over his subjects, in distinction of the "natural person," the one who "owns" his words and his actions.[3] Since the person, because of its rational component, has received the ability to choose for itself the right or the wrong conduct, its political meaning must necessarily transform the moral dimension of that option.

In civil society individuals are supposed to act according to their interests, while they delegate to the Law the limits to do damage to each other. Beginning with Vitoria, theologians and political writers investigated the contractual nature of political power in order to validate the formation of a private sphere in which the subjects acted in terms of will and from a rationalization of their interests. In the field of Law, this process will produce the conceptualization of "subjective rights" as a faculty of the people (the Right), as opposed to the "objective rights" that emanate from the State (the Law).[4]

The bourgeois state will assign to the full development of civil society the "differentiation" of labor and production, while morality may influence political decisions on the basis of conscience, but never on the basis of a principle. For the only principle that a political option should follow is the right or the wrong in terms of goals.

Of course, goals will vary dramatically whether the ruler sets them or rather they are set by representatives or by the people. Suárez never questions the authority of the king, but he emphasizes the contractual nature of his authority, a contract that God has designed and cannot be broken. In this way, the political and moral considerations of power do not depart from each other; on the contrary they maintain, according to Vázquez de Menchaca, a harmonious balance: "el derecho canónico y el civil proceden, por regla

---

[2] See my discussion of these issues in chapters 2 and 4.
[3] Hobbes, *Leviathan*, 111-121. In chapter 2, I comment this notion in relation to Gracián's ideas on the sovereignty of the person.
[4] See Annabel Brett, *Liberty, Right and Nature. Individual Rights in Later Scholastic Thought*, where she analyzes at length the work of Vázquez de Menchaca.

general, en perfecta unión y armonía." (Vázquez de Menchaca IV 384) (generally, canonical law and civil law proceed with a perfect union and harmony).

Both sets of laws, however, have different origins and, most important, they suppose different bodies of legislation and different interpreters. While canon law refers to the teachings of the Church and is said to rest on the "canonists" –the interpreters of the Fathers–, the civil law is the customary enforcement of laws for the protection of society and rests on society itself. The society of the "city" is, then, the outcome of the thrust to further the convenience of its members and, therefore, individuals are subjected to civil law only when somebody else claims a damage. Commenting on Vázquez de Menchaca, Brett sees that the Spanish jurist disengages the individual from moral obligations at the moment of civil conflicts:

> The citizens, then, are not morally bound to the city and to the keeping of its laws. This has two consequences: firstly, the contingency of any one individual's membership of a city; secondly, the contingency of the city itself. (Brett 201)

The important thing, in my view, is the relative separation of the fundamentals of natural law from the "historical" evolution of the forms of subjection to the State. This is something demanded by the emergence of the bourgeoisie as a class with a self-understanding of the origins of its own constitution. The separation from the Church's political doctrines was a necessary condition to deepen into the distinctive features of a legal structure in which the individual may be considered to be free to face his social options, particularly his economic options. The sense of "duty" that natural law theory supposedly instilled in the individual was a constriction to the self-regulatory capacity of all people to look for their own sense of good and well being. In the bourgeois civil society moral duty will become a matter of conscience that cannot enter the concrete contractual arrangements of individuals with opposing interests.

In the same vein, Suárez established a division between communal property under natural law and private property under positive, historical law. This division had already been established by medieval Scholastic doctrines as a reflection of the relative privatization of property in the Late Middle Ages. Going further, Suárez throws communal property, and probably natural law itself, back to the state of mankind before the Biblical Fall. The historical human being, he argues, is not constituted in such a way; on the contrary, private property is the inherent organization of human society and there is nothing in natural law –in the pre-historical essence of this society– that opposes it:

> division of property is better adapted to (human) nature in the fallen state [. . .] it is adapted to the existing state and condition of mankind [. . .] a division of property is not contrary to positive natural law; for there was no natural precept to forbid the making of such a division. (Suárez 276)

We face, then, the same as-a-matter-of-fact approach which, at the level of international politics, Vázquez de Menchaca took to justify his position that the theorization of power relations do not come from theoretical principles, but from the actual configuration of forces. Moreover, they also say that principles do not explain the functioning of society, particularly when those principles intended to rule rather than describe. The "real" society is the society of private interests and not the society of communal duties. Langholm has amply analyzed the contribution of late Scholastic thought to the debates over the philosophical arguments regarding the moral status of the agent of economic (private) dealings. According to Langholm, a crucial shift occurred when economic need in a particular dealing was no longer thought of as exercising a moral coercion over the individual; instead of lamenting the lack of willingness from the part of the needed, they declared that someone in need was still free to chose either to accept a bad deal, or find something better somewhere else.[5]

As a result, freedom of movement becomes an essential condition of an emergent civil society, as it is the conception of private property as a positive right and not as a "delegated" property:

> It is in the theory of property, however, that the natural rights tradition touches upon economics. Citizens' rights include, and in some authors are presented as mainly consisting of, property rights. [. . .] Following Aristotle, as well as several other ancient

---

[5] See the well-informed chapters 3 and 4 of his *The Legacy of Scholasticism in Economic Thought. Antecedents of Choice and Power.*

sources, the medieval masters explained the institution of private property as a means to avoid strife and inefficient use of common resources, as well as, according to a typical suggestion by Thomas Aquinas, social disorder. Aquinas saw this institution in terms of an addition to natural law, which originally decreed community of property [. . .] Medieval scholastic property theory, while acknowledging limited private rights as the most feasible practical arrangement, was thus essentially duty oriented. Suárez does not break with Aquinas but shifts his emphasis from a duty to share to a right to claim and keep. Under the original condition of common ownership, natural law decreed that no one should be prevented from making the necessary use of common property. Under present condition, when property is divided, the natural law forbids the taking of what belongs to another. (Langholm, *The legacy of Scholasticism* 166)

Like the *arbitristas* (writers of economic issues) will do in innumerable occasions, a political theorist such Vázquez de Menchaca attacked the system of taxation because it enriched a few people at the expenses of many productive and poor people. The attack is in many cases directed against the hierarchies of the Church:

mas si deseas saber a qué fines o a qué obras se destinan esas recaudaciones de dinero que en la mayor parte de los casos se exigen a personas miserables, te lo diré en pocas palabras: para que tan inmensos recursos y riquezas vayan todos a parar a manos de esos prelados y crezca aún más el cúmulo de sus bienes. Y de ahí ¿qué se seguirá? Que compren y acaparen las propiedades todas de los necesitados, los sembrados y los campos, censos y rentas aunas, y en una palabra todos los bienes, fortunas y patrimonios, para darlos o dejarlos en herencia a sus hijos o nietos; de este modo los bienes que servían para aliviar la vida de tantos miles de personas, van a parar a poder de unos pocos. (Vázquez de Menchaca I, 193)

(if you wish to know what goals or works are funded with these collections of money that are taken mostly from very poor persons, I will tell you in a few words: such immense resources and wealth end in the hands of those prelates so their accumulation of property will grow even more. And then, what follows? That they buy and monopolize all the properties of the needy, sown fields and lands, private debts and rents, in short all properties, fortunes and patrimonies, so they can give them or pass them on to their sons and grandsons; in this way the property that alleviated the suffering of so many thousands of persons, ends in the hands of a few.

The fight on the part of jurists and political economists against privileges shows the degree of development of a bourgeois thought committed to investigating the state of an economic society, this is the *república*. The analysis of concrete relations among nations and people went hand in hand with the re-thinking of the way the concrete legal development made a qualitative change in relation to the a-historical natural law. The fight was therefore, at many points, a fight against the privileges of the Church:

> la obligación de pagar diezmos es sólo de derecho positivo, no de derecho natural o divino, luego en virtud del mismo derecho podrán desaparecer y ser desterrados. (Vázquez de Menchaca IV, 414)
>
> (the obligation to pay 'diezmos' [Church's taxes] does not belong to natural or divine law but only to positive law, thus according to this law 'diezmos' can disappear and be banned.)

Some years later, González de Cellorigo, Fernández de Navarrete, Sancho de Moncada, López Bravo, Caxa de Leruela, and many others will articulate from different angles the same reformist project. The development of a civil society had to acquire a higher level of social and economic justice in order to rationalize the productive resources and strengthen a "national" cohesion.

Luis Ortiz's pioneer work (1558) on the state of commerce provides a clear image of the beginnings of this national sense in the concept of the *república*:

> Y si se mandase que ningunas personas, de cualquier estado y condiçión que sean, no traxesen sino paño sin guarniçión, o seda sin guarniçión, bernán dello ynnumerables prouechos al Reyno, y lo prinçipal que la rrepública se afiçionará a otros ofiçios fuera de los dichos... (Ortiz 125)
>
> (If it were ordered that any person of any status and condition wear wool without ornaments, or silk without ornaments, numerous advantages would come to the kingdom, and above all

the republic would develop other jobs instead of the ones mentioned)

Ortiz underlines the differences between estates, the kingdom and the *república* as pertaining to different spheres of the social life. While the estates obviously refer to the traditional separation of economic groups by privileges, and the kingdom refers to the political *dominium* of the Monarchy, the *república* points to a sphere determined above all by economic exchanges. This *república* seems to convey the idea of an emergent society established for the pursuit and accumulation of wealth if proper conditions are met:

> en muchos pueblos de Flandes y de otros estraños, biendo la desorden que otros tiempos a auido en lo de los trajes, tienen hechas ordenanças con que no sólo conserban sus rrepúblicas, mas banlas acreçentando en grande rriqueza. (Ortiz 126)

> (in many towns of Flandes and other foreign places, considering the lack of order in previous years regarding clothing, they have made rules that not only permit the conservation of their republics, but also the increase of their wealth.)

Clearly, the *república* belongs to the sphere of wealth as an area independently conceived from the sphere of political subordination. This emergent civil society is properly understood as existing in a process of becoming and, therefore, it is not detached from the local circumscription where the actual economic exchange (buying and selling) takes place:

> en muchas prouinçias donde tienen buena orden y poliçia en el bibir, an hecho leyes de que an redundado grandes bienes a sus rrepúblicas. (Ortiz 125)

> (in many provinces with order and control in the way they live, they have made laws that have produced great benefits for their republics.)

Unlike the kingdom, however, the *república* is not reduced to the geographical territory where groups and "estates" are subjects of the Monarchy; rather they are economically related to these territories in so far as they pursue the attainment of wealth. Ortiz perceives the differentiation between the subordination of all subjects to the Monarchy, on the one hand, and the private relations of "all estates of people" in the *república*, on the other.

This is the notion of an emergent bourgeois society that many political economists and reformers might have had in mind when they analyzed the socio-economic conditions of Spanish (Castilian) society and proposed their nationalist and mercantile solutions to be ideally enforced by the king. These writers may well be considered the intellectual expression of the economic interests of the nascent bourgeoisie, as they clearly separated themselves from both the interests of the Church and the rentiers, and as they progressively developed an idea of civil society to cover national economic processes.[6]

The reformist project articulated the intellectual dynamics of the bourgeoisie, even though the development of the class had to face the economic and cultural circumstances of the imperialist and con-federal project of the Habsburgs and the privileged classes that supported them, in Spain as well as in central Europe. The project, however, was able to aspire at certain times to the administration of the Monarchy. The government of the Count-Duke of Olivares aimed at imposing a unifying political structure and at intervening in the promotion of state-run merchant companies. Olivares himself wrote *memoriales* to communicate his vision of the direction the Monarchy should take. In one of them he describes the general structure of Spanish society and, at one point, addresses the negative influence that the economic role of the Church exercises in the country:

> De manera, señor, que lo que se me ofrece advertir a V. Majd. en esto del brazo eclesiástico es que es el más rico de los reinos de V. Majd. y que lleva camino de ser dueño de todo, que es punto de graves inconvenientes hoy, que adelante se reconoce que podría ser la destrucción dellos. (Olivares 51)
>
> (So, my Lord, that what I have to warn Y.M. regarding the ecclesiastical arm is that it is the wealthiest in all kingdoms of Y.M., and that it is on the way to becoming the owner of everything,

---

[6] See Maravall's *Estado moderno y mentalidad social* (I, 467-473) for a discussion of a national feeling ("un sentimiento de nación") along the process of the construction of the Absolutist State.

which is an issue today of serious inconveniences, and that it is known that in the future it could mean the destruction of all of them.)

Olivares's reformist projects intended to negotiate a viable solution to the economic and political crisis of the Monarchy that could count on the support of some sectors of the traditional powers, in Castile and in the other kingdoms.[7] The goal was, however, to reform the economic structure of Spain, to dedicate the State to the tasks of mercantile rationalization and to compete with the other European powers that, in his view, were leading the world:

> Gobernar por compañías y consulados la mercancía de España, poniendo el hombro en reducir los españoles a mercaderes. Este es el camino, señor, que puede resucitar la Monarquía de V. Majd., y con gobernar bien éste se han hecho poderosos nuestros enemigos, conquistan con él el del mundo, y no corriendo por su cuenta el despacho de los galeones de V. Majd. gozan en ellos incomparables sumas de las que vienen para V. Majd. y sus fieles vasallos. (Olivares 98)

> (To rule the Spanish merchandise through companies and consulates, forcing the Spaniards to become merchants. This is the way, my Lord, that can invigorate the Monarchy of Y.M.; for with this good government our enemies have become powerful and in this way they conquer the world, and without expending on the costs of the ships of Y.M., they benefit from the immense fortunes coming to Y.M. and faithful subjects.)

In their basic assumption, Olivares's ideas participated in the project of many political economists devoted to the expansion of a merchant capital. In this way, it expressed many of the dreams of the Castilian bourgeoisie. The intellectual dimension of these concerns expressly intended to conceptualize the feeling of confrontation against what seemed to be at the economic and cultural roots of all the wrong policies: the alliance, under the imperial ambition of the Monarchy, of the Church and the rentier class:

> Después de Villalar (1521), con la derrota de los comuneros no había quedado extinguida la actitud de discrepancia e, incluso,

---

[7] See Elliott, *The Count-Duke of Olivares*, particularly pp. 278-307.

de franca oposición a las líneas de gobierno que la monarquía de los Austrias fue siguiendo durante casi dos siglos, política que sufrió importantes cambios de dirección, pero que no por eso dejó de suscitar en todo momento críticas y lamentaciones. (Maravall, *La oposición política bajo los Austrias* 213)

(After Villalar [1521] the comuneros's defeat did not extinguish the dissident and even straightforward opposition to the policies that the government of the Austrian monarchy followed for almost two centuries; these policies experienced major changes, but never stopped provoking complaints and protests.)

Even more than political criticism, the conjuncture produced a reconsideration of the intellectual role of writing. Political as well as theological and economic writers envisioned a field of their own for their intellectual work, a field that was, in a still vague but decisive manner, the field of the *república*. This civil society could never be the result of the universalism of the Church, nor it could accept the order of an international Monarchy too promptly to spend the kingdom's wealth in maintaining foreign interventions and privileges. Civil society had to be a national society.

The controversies on the political status of the Indies, on poverty and on the economic illness of Castile were carried out almost in a vertiginous progression one after the other, as if they were the themes that set the stage for a national debate. The controversies resemble a search for a rationalization of productive resources and a reconsideration of the role of the Monarchy in a national-oriented economy.

The debates also witnessed major discrepancies regarding the interpretation of Christian orthodoxy in matters of spirituality as well as in matters of politics, economics and social reform. For Baeck, the theologians of the school of Salamanca were instrumental in the formation of intellectuals for whom the Christian tradition reached farsighted political overtones:

> In their moral and political philosophy they may be called democratic humanists. More than medieval schoolmen, they strongly emphasized the social and political autonomy of people in their role as citizens. They viewed humans as God's co-workers in the earthly realization of the divine plan. [. . .] The Salamancan theology gives the free will and the responsible conscience of the in-

dividual a prominent place. It culminates in the concept of a social pact between the authorities and the people. In its natural law theory, the people's sovereignty and the rights of the individual are recognized and stressed against the power of the feudal order, against imperial absolutism and even against the authority of the Church. (Baeck 184)

The political-economists, on the other hand, finally realized the open turn in favor of change and transformation of the political alliance in power:

> Their pamphleteering took issue with the structural inconsistencies of Spain's economic development. This inward looking analysis emphasized the functioning of the real sectors of the economy and marked a clear departure from monetary analysis. In their pamphlets and briefs to the court, they offered precepts for the reform of agriculture, rural exodus, urban unemployment, import substitution, a more positive work ethos, etc. Seen from the political angle, one could also call them the intellectual constituency of the nationalist bourgeoisie of Castile, in opposition to the tenets of the imperial party. (Baeck 182)

The debates on the *república* would eventually center on the theme of labor and the flow of merchandise in and out of the country. From the beginning of the discussions on poverty, these issues configured the central core of the reformist writing, as I show below in this chapter. The explicit goal of the bourgeois intellectuals was to strengthen an alliance between commerce and productive consumption. This alliance would result in an ethical compromise with the objectives of social mobility and spiritual freedom. Moreover, this ethical dimension enabled these writers to satisfy their need to show a cultural discrepancy with the official policies while reinforcing, according to them, a Christian legacy. This was a legacy that appealed for a consideration the role of the person in secular matters.

In the arena of international politics during the transformation of the feudal system, the relations between nations were still dominated by a close identification between the "representatives" and the interested parties of the kingdoms. Representatives and officials who belonged to the privileged classes executed political decisions, diplomatic efforts and military strategies, all in the name of the

Monarchy. In this way the internal tensions of these decisions reflected a centrifugal force that appeared many times to work against the interests of a national Monarchy, as Olivares saw and tried to overcome without success.[8]

Under the bourgeois state the relations between nations will be based on agreements of formal principles that will supposedly be executed by representatives of the (national) society. In the Early Modern period, the demarcation of the public function of these people (the representatives) was obscured by the fact that the public function of the privileged classes was also the "inherited" function of their class-identity.[9] This is a phenomenon related with the so-called process of "aristocratization," the drive by some members of the bourgeoisie to attain public positions and the lifestyle that accompanied the higher echelons of the Administration of the imperial Monarchy.[10]

The absolute need to establish the sphere of the private self as a realm of individual freedom was the radical feature of the writers who offered their work as a cultural intervention in their emergent civil society. A civil society constituted by the private dealings and private contracts of private individuals imposed upon their members the task of finding a high moral code with which to confront the wrongdoings done in the *república*.

---

[8] This is the case, for instance, of Olivares's proposal to create a national army as a means to alleviate the tax contribution of Castile. See Elliott 244-77.

[9] Public representation is one of the issues involved in the transformation of the "category" of the "public" from its origins in the sphere of power display to the sphere of the representation of civil society. From representing the State to representing the bourgeois society, Habermas follows major "structural" transformations of the "public sphere." He sees one of the major conflicts in the transformation of the "public" opposed to the "common" (State versus society] into the public opposed to the "private" (political sphere versus economic sphere). See his *The Structural Transformation of the Public Sphere*, particularly pp. 1-88.

[10] These phenomena exemplify, according to Maravall, the reinforcement of a seigniorial system of privileges. As a result of the economic crises, these privileges were seen in danger of dissolution and the regime attempted to dismantle the expectations of social mobility nurtured during the Renaissance (see his essay "From the Renaissance to the Baroque. The Diphasic Scheme of a Social Crisis," where he synthesizes his notion of the Baroque as a "conservative culture" developed at length in *The Culture of the Baroque. Analysis of a Historical Structure*). See also Atienza for a particular study of the growing monopoly of the nobility in the State's institutions during the first decades of the seventeenth century (*Aristocracia, poder y riqueza en la España moderna*). For a more theoretical discussion of the changing economic roles of capitalist classes in the face of an expanding or contracting market, see Wallerstein's discussions regarding "aristocratization" in "The Bourgeois(ie) as Concept and Reality."

Thus, some works of literature reflect the conjuncture of a fusion of economic discontent and a stricter appeal to moral and religious integrity. The ideological engagement with the lower classes in picaresque literature, for example, was the outcome of the controversies that shaped the articulation between the demand for a rationalized society in terms of productive resources, on the one hand, and the inquiry for a renovated Christian self, on the other.[11] This literary conjuncture articulated different aspects of the "national" debates by providing an integrative discourse to the literary society. They actualized concerns and issues that were treated at a more explicit political or ideological level in the writings of theologians and political economists.

The distinction between universal domination and the particular needs of a national kingdom may have been the political source of this new literary idea of personal self-determination. The contractual nature of power was seen as the means to attain a broader mobility for the flux of commerce. The self-determination of kingdoms had to result eventually in a further differentiation within social relationships, which substituted an individual economic agent for feudal-religious determinations.

The concern with productive consumption is the grounding force of the debates on poverty and, as such, it becomes the material basis for the discursive formation of a civil society, the *república*. The self-determination of this emergent bourgeois society appears as the progressive growth of local, regional and ideally national spaces are differentiated from the political space of the kingdom. These material spaces, intended for the free movement of people and economic exchange, would acquire unity by and through further accumulation of commercial and merchant capital.

The Wealth of the Republic

González de Cellorigo's esoteric *dictum* has become a common place in historical research. In the middle of his description of the causes of Spain's economic crisis around 1600, he states:

---

[11] This explains the force that Erasmian and Lutheran reformers had among urban, middle-class and professional people during the first half of the sixteenth century. See the classical study by Bataillon, *Erasmo y España*.

> Y llega a tanto que, por las constituciones de las órdenes militares, no puede tener hábito mercader ni tratante, que no parece sino que se han querido reducir estos Reinos a una República de hombres encantados que viven fuera del orden natural. (González de Cellorigo 79)

> (And it gets to the point where, by the decrees of the military orders, neither merchant nor dealer can join them, it appears that they have wanted to reduce these Kingdoms to a Republic of enchanted men who live outside the natural order.)

González de Cellorigo is criticizing the excessive value people place on *honra* –honor– and the low social esteem given to work, specifically agricultural work and commerce. It is worthwhile to note that Cellorigo situates his arguments within the context of the devastating human and economic consequences of the plague of 1596. Pérez Moreda has observed that:

> The plague of 1596-1602 resulted, therefore, in a socially selective rise in mortality. It was as if the rats and fleas had held back in the face of wealth and social standing. (Pérez Moreda 39)

Within the context of pauperization and economic decline, Cellorigo pointed at some specific reasons for the stagnation of labor and industry. Pierre Vilar, some years ago, undertook a socio-economic interpretation of the "time" of *Quixote* in which he related don Quijote's madness to González de Cellorigo's concerns with the evils of idleness, socio-psychological attempts of aristocratization, and disregard for productive activities at the threshold of Spain's seventeenth century.[12] In another place, González de Cellorigo states something that is even more illuminating, namely, that Spain has reached the nadir of bankruptcy:

---

[12] Vilar says: "Así en el declive de una sociedad gastada por la historia, en un país que ha llevado al punto más extremo sus contradicciones [. . .] en aquel momento surge una obra maestra que fija en imágenes el contraste tragicómico entre las superestructuras míticas y la realidad de las relaciones humanas." ("El tiempo del 'Quijote'" 345) (In a country which has taken to the most extreme point its contradictions [. . .] in that moment a masterpiece appears which fixes to images the tragicomic contrast between the mythic superstructures and the reality of human relationships.)

A muchos del Reino da que mirar el ver lo que las cosas de España señalan con tan contrarios efectos de lo que ellas en sí prometen, porque vemos al Rey más rico, más poderoso en todas suertes de riqueza y de grandeza, que España ni otra monarquía tuvieron y los vasallos en las mayores ocasiones de ser ricos, poderosos, hacendados, que ningún estado de República pudo alcanzar [. . .] y con todo ello no se halla en las historias que España haya llegado a mayor quiebra de la en que se ve. (González de Cellorigo 89)

(To many in the Kingdom seeing what the affairs of Spain point out with results so contrary to what they promise is grounds for suspicion, because we see the King richer, more powerful in all fortunes of wealth and grandeur, than Spain nor any other monarchy has had and the vassals with more opportunities to be rich, powerful, wealthy, than any Republican state could offer (. . .) yet in spite of all that one does not find in the histories that Spain has ever fallen into a deeper bankruptcy than the one in which it now finds itself.)

The major responsibility for having arrived at such a situation is, paradoxically, Spain's wealth: "lo que más ha hecho daño a estos Reinos es que las mismas riquezas que les han entrado son las que los han empobrecido." (*ibidem*) (What has most hurt these Kingdoms is that the same riches which have entered them are the very things which have impoverished them).

Spain is poor because it is rich.[13] Too much wealth in monetary terms has produced too much poverty. The people have given most of their energies to the trade of American gold and silver, for the exclusive purpose of accumulating values in the *censos* –investments in private debt– (50-51) with the result that differences between rich and poor have grown out of "proportion," (88-89) while commerce has been jeopardized:

---

[13] The economic paradoxes go on: "nunca tantos vasallos vio ricos como ahora hay, nunca tanta pobreza entre ellos, ni jamás Rey tan poderoso, ni de tantas rentas y Reinos, ni le ha habido hasta aquí que haya entrado a reinar que hallase tan disminuidos empeñados estados." (89-90) (At no time had so many rich subjects been seen as there are now, and at no time amid them so much poverty, nor a King so powerful, nor so many revenues and Kingdoms, nor until now a sovereign who beginning his reign discovered such diminished and debt-ridden states.)

> Y es que el mercader por el dulzor del seguro provecho de los censos deja sus tratos, el oficial desprecia su oficio, el labrador deja su labranza, el pastor su ganado, el noble vende sus tierras por trocar ciento que le valían por quinientos de juro, sin considerar que habiendo dado todos en este trato la renta firme de la heredad se acaba y el dinero se va en humo. Porque uno que labra ha de sustentar a sí y al señor de la heredad y al señor de la renta, y al cogedor del diezmo y al recaudador del censo y a los demás que piden, y de ahí arriba se puede hacer cuenta que de la poca gente que trabaja a la que huelga sale a razón de uno por treinta. (72)

> (And it's that the merchant because of the sweetness of the sure profit of the 'censos' abandons his business, the official looks down on his office, the farmer abandons his farm, the shepherd his flock, the nobleman sells his lands so as to exchange for a hundred what was certainly worth five hundred, without considering that having given all in the deal the steady income from the property ends and the money goes up in smoke. Because one who farms has to support oneself and the landowner and the taxgatherer, and the tithe-taker, and the debt collector and the rest who solicit, and in this way upwards it can be calculated that the ratio between the few people who work and the idle is one in thirty.)

Cellorigo complains that the economy is driven by financial speculation and that working people are overburden by heavy taxation. In the same fashion, a few years later López Bravo was to link poverty to this speculation with rent.[14] Sancho de Moncada was to say that the poor paid more than the rich;[15] and Fernández de Navarrete blamed the plight of farmers and peasants to financial speculation, taxation, usury and artificial overpricing:

> todo lo que adquieren con sudor, lo consumen en la voraz polilla de los censos y en la paga de las mohatras y usuras, a que les compele las necesidades (. . .) para que con sus vejaciones se enriquezcan los escribanos y procuradores. (Fernández de Navarrete 532-33)

---

[14] López Bravo, 340.
[15] Moncada, 179.

(All that they [peasants and farmers] acquire through sweat they consume on the voracious clothes' moth that is the 'censos' and in paying for fraudulent sales and usuries, which necessity requires of them, so that by their maltreatment the notaries and attorneys enrich themselves).

Though the specific arguments varied, these political economists were all committed to articulating a defense of protectionist measures against imports in order to favor the development of "internal," so to speak "national" (essentially Castilian) commerce and industry. Sancho de Moncada, after exposing racist and xenophobic justifications against gypsies and other ethnic minorities, says that foreign monarchies and people are growing at the expense of Spain's people, [16] citing it as the reason for the lack of employment, increased imports, and social and economic idleness and speculation in Castile. [17] Still in 1630, Caxa de Leruela continues to see the relationship between financial speculation and economic dependency on foreign goods:

> La ociosidad [. . .] ha llamado en su favor a la industria, y negociación de extranjeros, que le cuida las inteligencias, le ajusta los tiempos, previene las ocasiones y todo lo dispone diestramente para el beneficio, y que ha abierto la puerta a las mercaderías de fuera, y defraudando al comercio los caudales de marca mayor, embebiéndolos en los censos, juros, vínculos y mayorazgos (reclinatorio de esta holgazanería). (Caxa de Leruela 54-55)

> (Slothfulness [. . .] has summoned trickery to its aid, and the business of foreign people, which looks after its abilities, adjusts the seasons, foresees the risks and dexterously disposes of everything for a profit, and which has opened the doors to outside merchandise, and defrauding commerce of the best fortunes, enthralling them to the 'censos,' perpetuities, entails and 'mayorazgos' [the couch of this idleness]).

---

[16] He says: "con los frutos del reino se sustentan extranjeros, y fuera justo se sustentaran nacionales." (Moncada 102) (the fruits of the kingdom enrich foreigners; national people are the ones who rightfully must be enriched.)

[17] *Ibid.*, 108-109.

The battle against imports will be a familiar topic during the seventeenth century. [18] The *arbitrista* Fernández de Navarrete asks for the prohibition on the import of wheat, [19] while Sancho de Moncada insists on the enforcement of laws which encourage the retention of raw materials in the country. [20] Both of them believe that these measures will curtail speculation by the idle classes, reduce unproductive expenditures and lessen vagrancy, poverty and even the breakdown of marriages.

However, the relation between speculation and poverty was something that Luis Ortiz already had pointed to around 1557. His memorandum is a petition for the implementation of protectionist policies aimed at increasing Castilian manufacturing. Arguing for his proposals, Ortiz says that the source of "world money" is Spain:

> Lo primero se a de considerar que la prinçipal fuente del dinero del mundo es España, así por lo que en ella naze como por lo que biene de Indias. (Ortiz 127)

> (The first thing to be considered is that the principal source of money in the world is Spain, both because of how much is from here and because of how much comes from the Indies.)

The money in the world comes to Europe from America. It does it through Spain, but it leaves her as Spain is decapitalized by the defeat of local industries. Ortiz has the clear understanding that competition among nations insures the circulation of money and argues that the king must provide for the increase of money in the kingdom and for the acquisition of foreign money: "no sólo se da

---

[18] Caxa even will go as far as to ask for a more explicit intervention of the State to reduce 'bienes vinculados' that is the system of 'mayorazgos' that blocked the selling of lands: "se deberían facilitar las licencias para enajenar bienes vinculados, hasta que se redujeran a cantidad, y número congruente a la razón de Estado de estos reinos." (*ibid*. 56) (permits must be given to alienate them in order to reduce them to the amount and number fitting the reason of the State of these kingdoms.) The fight for the abolition of 'mayorazgos,' we know, will be a lost cause until the XIX century. True, Caxa is here defending the owners grouped in the Mesta, who have seen their wood trade going down as a result of the crisis of Castilian wood industry, which in turn was the consequence of the consolidation of the financial-industrial complex of the United Provinces. Thus, his position against agricultural rent.

[19] Fernández de Navarrete, 535.
[20] Moncada, 105.

rremedio que no salgan dineros del rreyno, mas se probee que entre él de otros rreynos, todo o la mayor parte de lo que en ellos obiere." (146) (Not only is it prescribed as a cure that money should not leave the kingdom, but also that money from other kingdoms enter in it, all or the greater part of what in them existed).

It may be said, in general terms, that seventeenth-century *arbitristas* were concerned, above all, with the lack of productivity of Spain, while certain contemporaries of Ortiz, such as Vives, had in mind, first and foremost how to get rid of poverty in order to drive the economy. In both cases, however, all they were describing the progressive decapitalization of the Spanish monarchy.

The symptoms of this decapitalization appeared to be highly contradictory, since on the one hand, Spain was the first to receive in its ports and cities America's metals, and on the other these metals seemed to be somehow related to the spread of poverty and the stagnation of Castilian commerce. Hamilton argued that American metals caused a "revolution of prices" that, in turn, made possible a rapid increase of benefits for the capitalists by way of permanent decreases in salaries. Pierre Vilar, however, rather understood that the flow of gold and silver confronted the specific relations of production in Spain and in other parts of Europe, with the former becoming dependent on the industrial centers of the latter. [21] Some years before Vilar, Carande identified this decapitalization as the result of the State's debt first to German banks, then to Italian, which could only be alleviated by constant confiscation and increasing taxation. [22] More recently, Felipe Ruiz Martín has shown the devastating consequences of these policies on the Castilian bourgeoisie. [23] Also, Vassberg gives us a good account of this tax burden on Castilian peasants, [24] while for his part, Artola has pointed out that the complex system of taxation, especially with regard to collections,

---

[21] See his "Problems of the Formation of Capitalism," where he contested Hamilton 'inflationary' conception of the rise of capitalism (put forward in *American Treasure and the Price Revolution in Spain*) and advanced the idea of understanding Spain's stagnation as the result of its role in incorporating the American labor force within the European economy. See also his *A History of Gold and Money* for a larger picture of the movement of metals.

[22] In *Carlos V y sus banqueros*, especially volume 3, *Los caminos del oro y de la plata*.

[23] *Pequeño capitalismo. Gran capitalismo*, where he describes Castile's dependency on Genoese interests.

[24] *Land and Society in Golden Age Castile*, especially pp. 190-230.

resulted in a permanent creation of intermediaries who sought significant profits from the rent and investment of taxes, that is with the private investment of the State's incomes. By the second half of the seventeenth century: "we see the existence of a financial bourgeoisie with important economic resources and ample credit." ([se] permite descubrir la presencia de una burguesía financiera con importantes recursos económicos y amplio crédito.) (Artola 211)

Increasing taxation, increased poverty and increasing overvaluation of aristocratic ideals, such as honor, are reported by González de Cellorigo, Sancho de Moncada, Fernández de Navarrete and López Bravo who says:

> el dueño de un censo, el poseedor de un mayorazgo, el contertulio de la ociosidad literaria, el que fomenta el ocio ajeno o, lo que es peor, el sembrador o protagonista de pleitos o el maestro o ministro de cualquier tipo de engaño o desvergüenza, bien comido y vestido y acaso con lujo –puede alcanzar todos los honores. (López Bravo 261-2)

> (the owner of a "censo," the holder of a "mayorazgo," the fellow member of a useless literary circle, the one who encourages sloth in his neighbors, or, what is worse, the sower of or protagonist in disputes or the teacher or minister of whatever kind of trickery or shamelessness, well fed and dressed and perhaps living in luxury –can obtain all the positions.)

In his study on the transition to capitalism in Castile, Yun Casalilla qualifies the overall significance of the interrelation between debt and a "seigniorial figure" of this type of capitalist interested exclusively in financial speculation:

> la nobleza local, las oligarquías rectoras de las ciudades, los mercaderes y banqueros y los funcionarios enriquecidos a la sombra del Estado dedicaron una parte creciente de sus capitales a la constitución de censos sobre las rentas de mayorazgos y de juros sobre la Hacienda real. (Yun Casalilla 643)

> (the local nobility, the ruling oligarchies in the cities, the merchants and the bankers and the functionaries prospering in the shade of the State dedicated a growing part of their capital to the establishment of 'censos' on the revenues of 'mayorazgos' and on perpetuities on the Royal Treasury.)

The so-called aristocratization, the strengthening of seigniorial and ecclesiastical power in Spain was reported in the *Relaciones Topográficas* of 1575-1580, where at one point people complained about the *diezmos* –the Church's taxation–: "ya no se sabe si el estado es una forma de Iglesia o la Iglesia una forma de estado." (It is no longer known whether the state is a kind of church or the church a kind of state) [25] Salomon notes that the *Relaciones* mention expropriations of communal lands and small properties, and that large landowners, both noblemen and churchmen, lived solely on land rents from the area of New Castile. [26] More recently, Francis Brumont has concluded similar socio-economic consequences for the area of Old Castile, though the structure of ownership differed, the result of the crisis was: "enriquecimiento de ricos, emprobrecimiento de los más, aparición de más jornaleros y de más pobres." (Brumont 225-231) (The enrichment of the rich, the impoverishment of the majority, the appearance of more day laborers and more poor people.)

The increasing empowerment of the Church is the very reason why writers such as Fernández de Navarrete, López Bravo and, still in 1630, Caxa de Leruela warn against the extraordinary number of people choosing an ecclesiastical career, and against the opening of new convents. [27]

The crisis of Castilian commerce in the 1530's, the rapid spread of poverty and the so-called "typical" Spanish obsession with *honor*, led Cavillac to conclude that it was "the victory of financial capital" (el triunfo del capitalismo financiero) (Cavillac, "La problemática..." CXX). According to Wallerstein, this financial capital,

---

[25] In Noël Salomon, *La vida rural castellana en tiempos de Felipe II*, 223. Also Vassberg, in *La venta de tierras baldías...* follows up some cases of land confiscation and dispossession of small owners and the obligation imposed on some peasants to buy the lands in which they had been working for generations under communal or municipal ownership.

[26] *Ibid.*, 268 ff. and 320.

[27] López Bravo, 233-234; Fernández de Navarrete, 537. Caxa de Leruela says: "La retirada que han hecho muchos a los claustros y sacerdocio en España ha sido ocasionada de las miserias, trabajo, y necesidad del siglo. [. . .] El quedarse muchísimos acobardados sin estado, es efecto de la misma causa, en que no tiene poca parte la vanidad, reconociendo las dificultades que oprimen al matrimonio." (Caxa de Leruela, 61-2) (The retirement which many in Spain have made to the cloisters and the priesthood has been occasioned by the century's misery, toil, and hardship [. . .] the unwed state of many, is an effect of the same cause, in which vanity has played no small part, recognizing the difficulties which oppress matrimony.)

grounded on monetary speculation, was the consequence of a larger dynamic in which the Spanish –and Portuguese– empires were immersed in the development of capitalism.

In Wallerstein's analysis, Spain and Portugal took the first steps into the new system during the "short" sixteenth century, but they fell back during the "long" sixteenth century and finally they survived the seventeenth as peripheries of the core centers of capital accumulation in central Europe. In other words, their decadence was the result of a reorganization of capitalism that must break through any imperial conception of sovereignty, in favor of an economic system composed of free nations.[28]

Concerns with the circulation of wealth were closely connected to the debates on poverty and proposals to eradicate and/or control it.[29] Writers developed extensive views on the role of money. During the same period of time that initiates the collapse of the Spanish economy (the second half of the sixteenth century), major works appear on the question of money, profit and monetary investments.

Of course, the *memorialistas* –writers of memorials, essays addressed to the King or some other political institution– and the *arbitristas* in general also write on money. Ortiz's *Memorial* analyzes the relation between imports and circulation of money, and later López Bravo shows a clear understanding of its function in trade:

> el verdadero valor del dinero depende de su peso y calidad natural, sí; pero también de las mercancías que balancea, y tanto más vale el dinero, cuanto mayor es el número de mercancías que balancea, y tantas más balancea cuantas más afluyen. (López Bravo 332)
>
> (The true value of money depends on its weight and natural quality, yes; but also on the commodities which it balances, and

---

[28] *The Modern World-System*. During the seventeenth century, what Spain faces is the loss of the struggle for political hegemony in Europe, the economic hegemony having already been lost during the "long" sixteenth century.

[29] For a description of these debates see Linda Martz, *Poverty and Welfare in Habsburg Spain. The Example of Toledo*, particularly pp. 7-91; and Anne Cruz, *Discourses of Poverty: Social Reform and the Picaresque Novel in Early Modern Spain*, particularly pp. 21-29 and 39-74. In the first two chapters of his *La literatura picaresca desde la historia social*, Maravall traces the changes in the conception of poverty, from the Medieval idea of the "religious" role of the poor, to the modern, secular and urban-centered, understanding of poverty as a social disease. Cavillac's essay, mentioned, is a seminal work on the issue.

the value of the money increases when it balances a greater number of commodities, and it balances more the more the commodities flow.)

As we have seen, however, Ortiz, López Bravo, Sancho de Moncada, González de Cellorigo, Fernández de Navarrete and Caxa de Leruela intended to promote mercantilist policies to ignite "national" production. They had in mind, loosely speaking, an *idearium* grounded in Castilian mercantile capital which was jeopardized by the decapitalization brought about by Spain's dependency on European manufacturers and the permanent increase of private and public debts. [30] These political economists paid attention to what later Marx saw as the rule of primitive accumulation in the relation between monetary speculation and the negative appearance of wealth in debt:

> The only part of the so-called national wealth that actually enters into the collective possession of a modern nation is –the national debt [. . .] Public credit becomes the *credo* of Capital [. . .] The public debt becomes one of the most powerful levers of primitive accumulation. As with the stroke of an enchanter's wand, it endows unproductive money with the power of creation and it turns it into capital, without forcing it to expose itself to the trouble and risks inseparable from its employment in industry or even usury. The state's creditors actually give nothing away, for the sum lent is transformed into public bonds, easily negotiable, which go on functioning in their hands just as so much hard cash would. But furthermore, and quite apart from the class of idle *rentiers* thus created, the improvised wealth of the financiers who play the role of middlemen between the government and the nation (. . .) the national debt has given rise to joint-stock companies, to dealings in negotiable effects of all kinds, and to speculation: in a word, it has given rise to stock-exchange gambling and the modern bankocracy. (Marx 919)

Moreover, there were moral economists who, following basically Scholastic doctrine, were able to give a very broad and complete

---

[30] "Pues cuanto oro, y plata, entra de las Indias parece tesoro de duendes, y que el mismo viento, que lo trae, lo lleva." (Caxa de Leruela 38) (Because all the gold, and silver, which enters from the Indies, seems like an enchanted treasure in that the same winds which bring it in, take it out.)

picture of the circulation and accumulation of money and, therefore, unintentionally, of the accumulation of capital. Following well-established interpretations of Aristotle's idea of money, Tomás de Mercado writes around 1569:

> En ninguna parte, en ninguna ocasión, se apreció jamás cosa según su natural, sino por nuestra necesidad y uso. Hasta en los metales y en la misma moneda, el oro, plata, piedras y perlas, que es lo sumo de todo Oriente y Occidente de este viejo mundo, en ninguna provincia ni reino del nuevo que llamamos Indias tuvo tanta reputación, y en muchos de ellos no tiene aún el día de hoy ninguna. (Mercado 96)

> (Never, at no time, was a thing ever valued according to its nature, rather as a result of our needs and uses. Even with the metals and in the coin itself, gold, silver, stones and pearls, which are the sum of all the Orient and Occident of this old world, and in no province or kingdom of the new which we call Indies had it ever so great a reputation, and in many parts of them it still does not have any today.)

The question is not just that Spain can extract gold and silver and take them to Europe; the question, obviously, is that the value of money is a specific social value. Since its value is socially determined, the issue that follows is to question how and why there is a real variation of that value. Tomás de Mercado, as well as many of the other economists of the "School of Salamanca," were trained theologians and their concerns were preceptive in nature:

> "De arte que la justicia que en todos los contratos es la igualdad que en ellos se ha de hacer, a lo cual —como extensamente probamos— nos obliga no sólo la ley divina, sino también la misma ley natural." (*ibid.* 55)

> (What is just is equality in the contracts, to which —as we extensively prove— not only divine law but also natural law itself obligates us.)

This preceptive and Thomist consideration was related to an interest against foreign intervention in internal trade: "cuando quisiere por buenos respectos traer de fuera y vender alguna mercadería, no venda ni dé en ninguna manera a ningún particular este privilegio (. . .) sino ponga sus oficiales [of the State] que lo tengan y ejerciten." (*ibidem*, 95) [31] (When you would like for good reasons to bring from outside and sell some merchandise, do not by any means sell this privilege to just anyone [. . .] but have your officials set it and apply it.)

Looking after justice and equality in economic dealings has been the official theological position. It was supposedly based on an interpretation of Aristotle's writings on money, or "chrematistics," the search for the principle of proportion in the economic (originally household business). However, though being theological or moral, the intent of these economists was to give a general and, sometimes very specific description of the market, as well as the first modern analysis of the formation of value in exchange.

Pierre Vilar noted that both groups of writers, the political economists and the moral economists, shared the same view of the problem, though with a difference in approach:

> No se puede confundir el camino intelectual recorrido por los doctores-confesores con el recorrido por los "políticos" autores de "memoriales." Los primeros esbozan una teoría de los precios tras meditar sobre los cambios, ya que se plantean el problema individual de la legitimidad de las ganancias; entran de lleno en la vía del subjetivismo psicológico, del análisis microeconómico, del equilibrio. Los segundos se plantean preguntas sobre la economía global, sobre la hacienda real; están en la vía de la "contabilidad nacional." (Vilar, *Crecimiento y desarrollo* 145) [32]

(The intellectual path travelled by father confessors cannot be confused with the one traveled by the "political" authors of "memoriales." The former outline a theory of prices after pondering about exchange rates, since they pose the individual problem of the legitimacy of profits, they enter entirely on the route to psychological subjectivism, and microeconomic analysis, of balance. The latter pose questions concerning the global econ-

---

[31] It is worth noting that Castilian trade with America is considered by Mercado to be part of the "internal" as opposed to the foreign trade.

[32] In this study, Vilar shows how these writers argued against the export of metals because it was the consequence of the lack of national wealth, and not because their monetary thinking was founded on the idea that wealth was equivalent to the amount of money in circulation. Vid. also Grice-Hutchinson, "Contributions of the School of Salamanca to Monetary Theory as a Result of the Discovery of the New World."

omy, concerning the Royal treasury; they are on the route of "national accountancy.")

Mercado, for example, describes the increase in value of some commodities in American trade as a result of these commodities being paid for in the colonies, though the sale is realized in Spain:

> Por lo cual es injusto que, vendiéndose aquí la mercadería o vino, se pague como vale en Nueva España por remitirse allá la paga, porque realmente sólo tiene en cuenta con la necesidad presente del que compra. Y así excede muchas veces no solamente al doble y tres doble al precio verdadero y corriente, más aun al de las Indias. (Mercado 194)

> (Because of this it is unfair that, selling here [in Spain] the merchandise or wine, one pays what it is worth in New Spain so as to remit the pay there, because really this only takes into account the needs of the one who buys. And in this way the price exceeds many times over not only double and triple the real and current price, but still more that of the Indies.)

We can see here the creation of a value in circulation which has to do with the increase of price, that is, as Marx would put it, with merely an increase in the form or the "name" of the universal equivalent of exchange, money.[33]

These ghostly fluctuations of value corresponded to the concrete circumstances of the local markets, of course, and the need of many entrepreneurs to have rapid access to cash. For example, another transaction that these moralists considered to be wrong was the *barata*, the selling by credit, at a higher price, to someone who, because of his financial needs, will have to resell in cash at a lower price.[34]

This debt chain will be the standard situation of Spain's capital as well as of the State's treasury, because, at the level of large-scale trade, it was mainly foreign banks and financial companies which

---

[33] *Capital* I, 162-163; 195-198.
[34] Tomás de Mercado, *ibidem*, 240. The question of the cash-flow as one of the determinant circumstances in the accumulation of continental financial capital through American trade, is analyzed by Wallerstein, cited, and before him by Ferdinand Braudel, in *Civilization and Capitalism*, more extensively in volume 2, *The Wheels of Commerce*.

were the only ones able to afford large sums of money. The internationalization of the financial system is already described by Mercado:

> Tienen contratación en todas las partes de la cristiandad y aun en Berbería. A Flandes cargan lanas, aceites y bastardos; de allá traen todo género de mercería, tapicería, librería. A Florencia envían cochinilla, cueros; traen oro hilado, brocados, seda y, de todas aquellas partes, gran multitud de lienzos. En Cabo Verde tienen el trato de los negros, negocio de gran caudal y mucho interés. A todas las Indias envían grandes cargazones de toda suerte de ropa; traen de allá oro, plata, perlas, grana y cueros, en grandísima cantidad. Item, para asegurar lo que cargan, que son millones de valor, tienen necesidad de asegurar en Lisboa, en Burgos, en Lyon de Francia, Flandes, porque es tan gran cantidad la que cargan que no bastan los de Sevilla, ni de veinte Sevillas, a asegurarlo. Los de Burgos tienen aquí sus factores que o cargan en su nombre o aseguran a los cargadores, o reciben o venden lo que de Flandes les traen. Los de Italia también han menester a los de aquí para los mismos efectos. De modo que cualquier mercader caudaloso trata el día de hoy en todas las partes del mundo y tiene personas que en todas ellas les correspondan, den crédito y fe a sus letras y las paguen, porque han menester dineros en todas ellas [. . .] De modo que cualquiera de éstos [. . .] tiene necesidad de tener dineros en todas partes o para comprar o pagar o cobrar, porque en todas deben y les deben. (Mercado 374-5)

> (They trade in every corner of Christendom and even in with the Moorish. To Flanders they carry wool, oils, and sails; from there they bring all sorts of wares, tapestries, books. To Florence they send cochineal, skins, they bring gold thread, brocades, silk, and from all those regions, a great many linens. In Cape Verde they have the slave trade, a business of great profit and benefit. To all parts of the Indies they send great cargos of all sorts of clothes; they bring from there gold, silver, pearls, grain and skins, in the greatest quantity. Furthermore, to insure what they carry, which is worth millions, they have necessity to receive payments in Lisbon, Burgos, Lyons in France, Flanders, because the quantity which they carry is so great that the ones of Seville are not enough, nor of twenty Sevilles, to insure it. Those from Burgos have here their agents who either carry in their name or insure the shippers, or receive or sell what they are brought from Flanders. Those from Italy also have need of those from here for the same money. So that any wealthy mer-

chant trades today in all parts of the world and has people who in all of them correspond with them, give credit and attest to their bills of payment and pay them, because they have need of money in all of them [. . .] so that any of these [. . .] has reason to have money in all parts or to buy or pay or charge, because everywhere they owe and are owed.)

After Mercado, and around 1590, the Jesuit Luis de Molina writes with greater specificity on the nature and circumstances of monetary dealings. Like Mercado, Molina is a moralist in the sense that, being also a theologian, his economic analysis is for him only a means to establish a moral justification for profit. He was concerned rather with the welfare of the *república*, and thus he emphasized, for instance, the intentions of people involved in any transaction in order to see whether those intentions were theologically correct. Following these assumptions, Molina investigated the transformation in value of money and capital, particularly in operations of credit, in order to distinguish usury, the lending of money with the intention of acquiring profit –morally condemned– from the rightful acquisition of gains. Like everyone in the Scholastic tradition, Molina is also looking for parity and equality in transactions, and thus a gain would be correct only as a payment for service and to pay back a possible economic injury that the lender would have by loaning out his money.[35]

In the same vein as that of the political economists, these Scholastic economists considered money to be a measure of value, and precisely because of that, an unproductive commodity. And like the *memorialistas*, the moralists related their concerns with financial speculation, rent, commodity imports and idleness to a social and cultural interpretation of the state of society.

---

[35] For a discussion of this issue, see Francisco Gómez-Camacho, Introduction to his edition of Molina's *Tratado sobre los préstamos y la usura* (c. 1597); for a broader analysis of Molina's nominalism in the measure of value in "time," also Gómez-Camacho's Introduction to Molina's *Tratado sobre los cambios*, mentioned, and Vilar's "Los primitivos españoles del pensamiento económico," also mentioned. For a discussion on the question of economic welfare in the Scholastic tradition and the 'public good' based in natural law, see Schumpeter, *History of Economic Analysis*, particularly pp. 96-115. For a study of the origins of the Scholastic interpretation of Aristotle's position on money, vid. Odd Langholm, *Wealth and Money in the Aristotelian Tradition*.

I have mentioned these few writings to point out that the sixteenth and seventeenth-century intellectual horizon represents an effort to map the major transformations in the foundations of the social and economic structures. My comments do not exhaust all the economic issues brought forward in these writings, nor do they encompass all the writers. My point is that this horizon concretized a discourse in which lack of capitalization and debt were the major junctures of analysis. To mention again Yun Casalilla, the emergence of capitalism was founded in:

> un sistema hacendístico y fiscal que, esto es lo importante, se convirtió al mismo tiempo en un pesado engranaje de extracción y distribución del producto social entre los poderosos [. . .] todo ello era fruto de un sistema que difícilmente podía generar riqueza y que se había convertido en una maquinaria de creación de pobres y de diferenciación social y económica. (Yun Casalilla 448)
>
> (an economic and fiscal system which, this is the important thing, was converted at the same time into a heavy gear of extraction and distribution of the social product between the powerful [. . .] all of that was the fruit of a system which with difficulty could generate wealth and which had changed into a machine creating poverty and social and economic differentiation.)

This social and economic differentiation under an Imperial monarchy crippled the development of a bourgeois society. By addressing the problem, however, political and economic literature clearly brought forward with the term *república* a space for the society of private dealings.

Working on finding solutions to economic imbalances and monetary irregularities, these writers conceptualized the breakdown of the marriage between domination and private economic exchanges. In literature this break would reinforce the representation of the autonomy of the economic needs of the person and of his social sovereignty.

The Literature of the *República*

Some literary works became the instrument of a circle of writers and readers to reflect on the way individuals acted according to their access to wealth or their aspirations to acquire it. The representation of the autonomy of economic needs would find in this literature the proper vehicle to reflect on and, to a certain extent, to produce a sensibility of the conflicts and ambiguities of the *república*.

The enterprise of this emerging literary *república* was nothing less than to work on a representational dimension of society, in order to provide a depiction of a secular interaction while pointing to and searching for the capacity of individual self-assertion. Some texts of what I shall call the literature of the *república* tended to play with the idea of "apparent" forms of conduct, trade, and moral values. The world seemed to acquire the fictitious quality of literature, in part because the literature of the emerging civil society included the economic need as one of the categories with which reality became problematic, deceptive and representational.

Practically at the end of our period of study, there is a satirical dialogue that expresses a literary sensibility regarding the financial world. Published in 1688, José de la Vega describes in *Confusión de confusiones* the settings and the functioning of a stock market.[36] The text begins by stating that the intention is to assess: "el estado de la India, la disposición de la Europa, y el juego de los accionistas." (de la Vega 66) (the state of the Indies, the disposition of Europe and the game of stock-brokers.)

There are many literary references throughout the work. At one point it mentions Don Quixote as a comic –*gracioso*– hero, and the third dialogue starts with Segismundo's words, from Calderón's *La vida es sueño* –"mísero de mí. Ay infelize"– to continue the monologue in a comic mood: "que si pago muriendo" ("if I pay while I die"). The idea is to describe the movement of the stock market as a plot of deception and disguise.

The *acciones* (the stocks) function as plays because in the market:

---

[36] The complete title accomplishes the idea of portraying the stock-market in literary terms: *Diálogos curiosos entre un filósofo, un mercader discreto y un accionista erudito. Describiendo el negocio de las acciones, su origen, su etimología, su realidad, su juego y su enredo.*

campean con inimitables realces las trazas, las entradas y salidas, los escondidos, las tapadas, las contiendas, los desafíos, las burlas, los dislates, los empeños, el apagarse las luces, el refinarse los engaños, las traiciones, los embustes, las tragedias. (de la Vega 156)

(the schemes, the entrances and exits, the hideouts, the cover-ups, the disputes, the challenges, the gibes, the absurdities, the pledges, the appeasements, the news, the refinement of the swindles, the betrayals, the fibs, the tragedies, all campaign with inimitable splendor.)

This theatrical expression seeks to cover all possible outcomes of the movement of stocks. Moreover, fiction becomes the constitutive characterization of the way this movement is perceived and acted upon by different actors. This feeling of "deception" or falsehood is also the consequence of a state of things in which the individual must be on guard for the action of other people: "Mirad que no deve [sic] dormir quien tiene enemigos." (61) (Remember that you must not sleep if you have enemies.) This is advice that could be read in many literary texts from 1600 onward.

To be awake is, then, to see the movement of people in their apparent disguise, with their apparent intentions, as Gracián further elucidated. "Acciones tienen algo de divinas" (stocks have something of a divine aspect) it is said at one point; it means that they appear everywhere, nobody knows how they arrive, where they come from, how they dress, etc. The movement produces the perception of something and the image of an activity. As I will argue in the following chapters in relation with the status of these appearances, Baltasar Gracián observes that this movement is intentionally conceived in all human dealings.

The *Confusión de confusiones* represents an economic activity with the language of literature. This explicit connection testifies in my view a relevant intersection between the *república* of money and value –the emerging bourgeois, civil society– and the *república* of fictitious writing. The literary characteristic of the stock market indicates the vaporous nature of the movement of investments and the fictional traits immersed in their actors and actions.

De la Vega's dialogue continues a tradition that stems from the Renaissance. At the end of the fifteenth century with *La Celestina* the depiction of monetary relations began to shape Spanish literature. It did so by showing the specific nature of social confrontation resulting from economic wealth, and by constituting individual conflicts around self-assertion in the pursuit of success.[37] Self-assertion transforms ideals of friendship and love into the means for the acquisition of goods and money. In Rojas's text we can detect a discourse of private interests running under the relations of mutual dependency, where expectations and desires coalesce in a provocative, unknown spirit of mercantile values. On the basis of this spirit these characters discover and realize their personal role as economic entities. These individuals assert their values along a discourse of growth and within a clear consciousness of exchange and risk.

Social interaction seems to acquire a representational characteristic analogous if not in many occasions identical to a state of falsehood. Rojas's dialogues –particularly the servants and Celestina's dialogues– are always pregnant with hidden intentions and deceptive messages, with momentary alliances which would certainly cause somebody else's harm. While in the monologues the individual faces a state of confusion and alienation, dialogues become the discursive space of a *negocio* (the negation of the *otium*), a business-oriented verbal action for the expression of desires and goals.

Explicit and implicit dialogues participate in the creation of literary texts when fictitious writing initiates a reconfiguration of the increasing autonomy of mercantile exchanges into a reflection on the world of appearances and the possibility of a personal legitimization within a seemingly precarious stability of the social identity. The literature of *pícaros*, in concrete, shows a paradigmatic development from an original form of personal authenticity and self-assertion to a dramatic reaction against it with a reinforcement of the seigniorial authority.

This development can be traced in terms of the representation of the character's voice and his place within the conflict between an aristocratic state of mind and an emerging bourgeois sensibility.

---

[37] Maravall understood the representation of class conflict in this text in relation to the emergence of new relations of dependency between masters and servants. Rodríguez-Puértolas saw the class conflict around the depiction of social resentment. In any case, the social confrontation is centered on economic wealth, which is for González-Echeverría the ground for the elaboration on sexual symbolism in terms of the "structures of commerce." Deyermond, too, accepted the primary importance of class division in the conception of the work.

The explicit assertion of economic need as the ground for personal reflection in works such as *Lazarillo* and *Guzmán de Alfarache* by Mateo Alemán becomes an excuse for depicting a state of insecurity and danger for the seigniorial order. The author of *Lazarillo* and Quevedo have different projects for their respective representations of poverty and different views on the narration of a life. As a matter of fact, Quevedo's *Buscón* is an exercise in linguistic virtuosity from the author and exemplary self-degradation from his character.

While in *Lazarillo* the economic need serves the purposes of the narrative to free the voice of the character from the constraints of lineage, in *Buscón* that same economic need makes it possible to demonstrate the essential hierarchy of the world in terms of birth. Lazarillo is born poor in order to show his highest value in comparison to the nobility; Pablos is born poor because he has no value but only a drive to be somebody else —a drive that he never attains except in the realm of "appearances."

As Francisco Rico observed, Lázaro's life does not have a continuation in Pablos's, but rather in Guzmán's. Alemán provides a complex representation of the economic need of somebody who is not born in poverty, but falls into poverty several times during his life. In clear distinction to Pablos, both Lazarillo and Guzmán are characters of a narrative that aims at explaining their lives in relation either to the dynamics of poverty —in the case of *Lazarillo*— or the horizon of enrichment —in the case of *Guzmán*. In *Buscón*, however, poverty is the essential station of people like Pablos, and enrichment is not exactly a problematic of his life but a wish that denounces a deformed identity. This denunciation takes place by the subordination of Pablos to a narrator that has the literary gesture of being Pablos himself. Pablos narrates his own subordination to the seigniorial structure and his own acceptance of the values that forbid his aspirations to be a nobleman.

The aristocratic mind reacts against the course open by the literature of the *república*, censuring aspirations of personal growth and subjugating the self-expression of a personal life to the demands of a normative conduct based on seigniorial stratification. In other words, the dynamics of poverty and wealth that Guzmán attempts at explaining through his own discourse on an irregular enrichment, becomes the world of "real" and "unreal" social identities in *Buscón* and the rest of the literature of *pícaros*.

An early relation of literature with a broader set of discourses and debates on wealth had to witness the question of poverty. *Lazarillo de Tormes* participates in these debates also by talking about the place of honor in the lower echelons of the nobility and by actualizing a highly idealistic conception of a good fame. Lázaro displays an idea of fame connected to bourgeois notions of merit and self-improvement, which in turn both signify a renunciation of a conception of fame associated to the aristocratic honor. Lazarillo's life may be a matter of fame because it represents an "unheard" event, an unprecedented case of social survival that merits to be rewarded by, at least, public recognition. It is unheard the story of a poor man coping with poverty as such, that is poverty as his daily horizon and as his motivation for change.

Anne Cruz has shown that, in spite of its ambiguity, the novel emerged at the time when debates on poverty were a familiar issue for readers seeking reform in the Church, others favoring a feudal-oriented conception of poverty, or those more inclined to a secular solution to vagrancy. She concludes:

> No matter how dissembling the pícaro's discourse or ambiguous the author's attitude, the picaresque narrative exposes to the reader the complex tensions that arose at the time between religious and secular values and the ensuing divergent ideologies on the impoverished and methods of poor relief. (Cruz 38)

Lazarillo tells how drives for economic improvement introduce changes in the perception of personal and social values that, in turn, affects the very constitution of individual feelings and expectations. After leaving behind the scarcity of rural poverty and the urban uncertainty with his mother, Lázaro learns about hunger. At the same time, he experiences the hypocrisy of laymen and clergy, which inflicts a suffering that somehow he will eventually manage to transform into a practical knowledge in order to arrive at a safe harbor, *cumbre de toda buena fortuna*. (peak of all fortunes.)

By representing different aspects of this poverty, and by ironically portraying the transition from ignorance to a cynical accommodation disengaged from accepted norms, *Lazarillo de Tormes* discloses a literary (fictitious) writing that drives to explain some conditions of economic "marginality" at the outset of the capitalist world.[38] The story inscribes economic need as the basic trait of the character; it is not merely the context in which Lázaro's life develops but, more substantially, economic need is the condition for the very constitution of the fiction.

Moreover, as Juan Carlos Rodríguez argues, this economic need imprints in the character a rupture with feudal dependency by asserting his self within and above the disorder of the world. His absolute dispossession becomes the seed for an emerging immanent view of this world that does not demand a solution of that disorder or a transcendent justification of it.[39] Rather on the contrary, *Lazarillo de Tormes* is constructed as an episodic articulation of moments of life, which are in essence sequential junctures that condense several realities within Lázaro's life and within the world around him. Religion, economic status and sexual propriety are all given as having their particular circumstance and their specific meaning. In this regard, Francisco Rico stated clearly:

> La pluralidad de significados, la ambigüedad y la ironía me parecen tan consustanciales al *Lazarillo*, que sólo me las explico como hijuelas de un amplio escepticismo [. . .] El relativismo, en la axiología como en la epistemología, es también un humanismo. "No hay valores: hay vidas, individuos", parecían enseñarnos las fortunas y adversidades de Lázaro. (Rico 57-59)

> (I think that the plurality of meaning, the ambiguity and the irony are all so essential to *Lazarillo*, that I can only explain them as a result of a wide skepticism [. . .] Relativism, both in axiology and epystemology, belongs to the Humanism. "There are no values: there are lives, individuals," Lázaro's fortunes and misfortunes seemed to teach us.]

All possible meanings become a world if the person acquires the key to understand the process by which the self may grow against

---

[38] "El *Lazarillo* es la primera novela moderna porque es el primer texto literario que muestra, tanto en su forma como en su contenido anecdótico, la presencia en la vida humana de las fuerzas que el modo de producción capitalista conjura." (Beverley 63) (*Lazarillo* is the first modern novel because it is the first literary text that shows, in form and content, the presence in human life of forces that the capitalistic mode of production contrives.) See Maiorino's notion of econo-poetics in his Introduction to the collective volume *The Picaresque. Tradition and Displacement*.

[39] See *La literatura del pobre*, where Rodríguez situates *Lazarillo* at the threshold of the bourgeois ideology.

deceptive and contradictory values. In other words, Lazarillo's self-assertion emerges through a relationship between epistemological and moral relativism, on the one hand, and an economic intuition regarding the horizon of human interaction, on the other. This intuition responds, according to Maravall, to a change in the perception of social mobility and its consequences in the development of expectations that tended to break with a traditional frame of values and hierarchies. An expanded geographical movement and an unprecedented circulation of money favored these expectations, which progressively included an emphasis on individual growth and on a society less subjected to seigniorial principles. Maravall concludes:

> We have, then –and it seems worthwhile to dwell on it– come upon a deep and serious crisis that is caused by uncontainable aspirations prompted by historical growth and by empowering of the individual; and these aspirations provoke a deterioration of the established system, inasmuch as this system has been viewed as impotent before the forces of change which are consolidated against it. ("From the Renaissance to the Baroque..." 20)

New social and economic expectations tended to disengage individuals both from their traditional forms of dependency and from the values associated with them. As a consequence of the new conditions of religious relativism and individual self-assertion, the intellectual world begun to emphasize a society structured according to the possession of wealth and money, that is a society of rich and poor. In addition to –and sometimes in place of– a moral concern, the poor and poverty became a political and an intellectual issue. They begun to be treated as economic problems in themselves, which could have implications for the *república*. Literature was, then, able to creatively mediate in this public concern by offering a fictional view of the state of an emerging civil society, its possibilities and its dangers.

In fictitious writing and other texts, the poor affect the orderly functioning of the world. Literary texts consider the subjective side of poverty, the potential of an economic condition to influence individual conduct and collective responses. In other words, the literature of the *república* teaches that poverty and wealth are also processes in the life of persons, a vision that differs greatly from an organicist and substantial understanding of the place of economic power in the structure of social strata. Maravall observes that in this context the perception of poverty and the poor has a negative characterization, in distinction to the religiously conceived "positive" attitude toward the poor in medieval societies. Poor and poverty are no longer signs of a divine organization of the world, but rather immediate threats to the orderly functioning of the kingdoms.[40]

Even within a productivist approach to poverty we find this negative attitude toward the poor in Juan Luis Vives, an exemplary defender of an early secular solution to poverty. He states that: "deben considerar [los pobres] primeramente que la pobreza se la envía Dios justísimo por un oculto juicio, aun para ellos muy sutil, pues les quita la ocasión de pecar." (*Del socorro de los pobres* 267) (they [the poor] should consider first that poverty is sent by the most just God for an undisclosed reason, still for them very subtle, for it takes away the chance to sin.)

Indeed, this hidden plan of God must be a very subtle one for Lazarillo to understand it. However, he has learnt the ironic nature of many religious acts and, by extension, the ironic dimension of many of the signs of social distinction and value. His mother advised him to be on the side of the "good people," and that is exactly what he has always intended, to be on the side of the means of acquiring money. To have money and to be a good person must probably be part of Lázaro's understanding of a desirable life, particularly after his encounters with the people that either hide their poverty or manipulate abusively the economic need of others.

Lázaro's self-affirmation reflects an original consideration of the social meaning of hypocrisy. At the end of his journey –or rather at the beginning of his writing– this meaning results in the transformation of its specifically moral rigor, in order to designate an autonomous and relative characteristic of individual deals. The moral dilemma of either *Vuesa Merced* or of Lázaro himself –the seeming acceptance of his wife's sexual relation with his protector, the archpriest– becomes an excuse to assert the priority of economic considerations in the evaluation of a life. A conflict of authority may

---

[40] Maravall insists that poverty increasingly becomes an independent status for the characterization of people, in opposition to the emerging definition of individuals according to their economic wealth. See in particular the first part of *La literatura picaresca desde la historia social*.

also run under this provocative justification of a "private" matter. The autonomy of economic reasons from sexual improprieties or from any other shameful conduct, may undoubtedly place Lazarillo's story under the scrutiny of a wider public responsibility.

In this sense, Gómez Moriana argued that Lazarillo is "the vicar of a true subject" (Gómez Moriana 65) accommodating his voice to dominant discourses. Certainly, Lázaro's pragmatism and moral relativism accommodates well with a justification of a *status quo*. His story, however, does not suppress but rather explains his decision to go on with "his business" above any other consideration. This is in fact an assertive conduct that could call for the intervention of the traditional authority demanding a correction according to feudal subordination.

Indeed, the reinforcement of a traditional mentality brought about in matters of religion by the Counter-Reformation will consolidate the aristocratic ideology regarding social inequalities. However, I want to argue that through this reaction there persists still the reality of a mercantile intellectual life. In Mateo Alemán's *Guzmán de Alfarache*, this intellectual life shows a high level of maturity that cannot at all be confused with an endorsement of the nobility. Alemán places his *pícaro* within a broader context of economic unrest and intellectual transformations, some of which have a direct impact in the aristocratic reaction within the literature of the *república*. The manifestations of a bourgeois sensibility must be accorded its proper condition of existence along invigorating seigniorial values.

Like many, if not all, political and moral economists, Felipe de Carrizales, in Cervantes' *El celoso extremeño*, wonders about the value of his silver bullion. He has become a rich man in America with the *inquieto trato de las mercancías* (the troublesome dealings with commodities) where he went after he spent his *hacienda y juventud en Europa*. (his capital and youth in Europe) He ponders, however, what the value of his metal really is, since he does not see any profitable activity in trade any more. Carrizales has a moment of intimate reflection:

> Contemplaba Carrizales en sus barras, no por miserable, porque en algunos años que fue soldado aprendió a ser liberal, sino en lo que había de hacer de ellas, a causa que tenerlas en ser era cosa infructuosa, y tenerlas en casa, cebo para los codiciosos y desper-

THE WEALTH AND THE LITERATURE OF THE *REPÚBLICA* 57

> tador para ladrones. [. . .] Por otra parte, consideraba que la estrecheza de su patria era mucha y la gente muy pobre, y que el irse a vivir a ella era ponerse por blanco de todas las importunidades que los pobres suelen dar al rico. (Cervantes II, 101-2)

> (Carrizales contemplated his bars [silver bullion], not out of miserliness, because in the years that he was a soldier he learned to be liberal, rather because of what to do with them, because having them in themselves was an unfruitful thing, and having them at home, bait for the covetous and an inspiration to thieves. [. . .] On the other hand, he considered that his country was in dire straits and the people very poor, and thus to move there was to become a target for all the importunities which the poor tend to give the rich.)

Carrizales does not see a way to keep his wealth safe, since in themselves, *en ser*, his bullion bars were worth nothing; moreover, being now a rich man he will become a target for the poor. Carrizales *contemplaba*, that is, he meditated upon his silver; but he does not do so because he was a *miserable* (miser), a cheap lover of silver, rather he is reflecting on his silver and by means of that meditation he describes for himself the social state of his country. Not surprisingly, Carrizales decides to diversify his silver in a *censo* in a bank in order to live on rents and to build a magnificent house:

> Compró un rico menaje para adornar la casa, de modo que por tapicerías, estrados, y doseles ricos mostraba ser de un gran señor; compró, asimismo, cuatro esclavas blancas, [. . .] dio parte de su hacienda a censo, sitada en diversas y buenas partes, otra puso en el banco, y quedóse con alguna, para lo que se ofreciese. (Cervantes II, 104)

> (He bought a rich set of furniture to adorn the house, so that with tapestries, furniture, rich curtains, he presented himself as an important nobleman; he bought, likewise, four white slaves [. . .] he invested part of his hacienda in a "censo," placed in diverse and good areas, another he put in the bank, and he kept some, for whatever came up.)

In his youth he wasted his capital, and now being an old man, he is one of those rich people living on money and flaunting it as an important nobleman. To round out his economic meditation, he decides to get married in order to secure his capital.[41]

While *La Celestina* observes the emergence of a monetary view of social relations, and *Lazarillo* is an ironical response to individual dispossession, the literary production at the turn of the seventeenth century focuses prominently on an articulation of economic insecurity through the fragmentary patches of an inner self. Alemán's Guzmán painfully finds out that economic competition is a struggle among individuals who would use any means necessary to deceive in order to acquire money. He has discovered that "no hay otra cordura ni otra ciencia en el mundo, sino mucho tener y más tener." (679) (there is no other wisdom or plan of study than to have more and much more) Monetary wealth replaces all other attributes and virtues of people.

At some point, Guzmán decides to study theology in order to make a living. As was the case for many people in literature and in reality, a scholastic career was a way to escape poverty or to secure a privileged position. I have quoted some political economists who saw the dangerous increase in the number of these people and its impact in the stagnation of production. Kagan has described the stagnation of the schooling system and the university as a whole, a consequence of both the seigniorial reaction against literacy and the consolidation of so-called orthodox Church doctrines in all areas of formal knowledge.[42] In Cervantes's *El licenciado Vidriera*, Tomás Rodaja confesses that he wants to study at the university level because he has heard that *de los hombres se hacen los obispos* (men may become bishops) but he dies fighting in a war in Flandes where he goes to make a living.[43]

Guzmán's two marriages are essentially businesses; the second one is even an economic enterprise, using his wife as a sexual commodity. As Rodríguez-Matos has nicely analyzed, Gracia –Guzmán's wife– becomes the means for his enrichment after he realizes that

---

[41] I have analyzed the relation between this unlucky marriage and the old man's economic fortune in *Lectura y representación. Análisis cultural de las 'Novelas ejemplares,'* pp. 112-131.

[42] See *Students and Society in Early Modern Spain*. Kagan gives an account of the decrease of financial support to popular literacy that goes hand in hand with the economic decline.

[43] See my analysis of this novel in *Lectura y representación*, cited above, where I argued that Cervantes is questioning in this novel the social function of reading and of formal education.

the Church is not a profitable place for him.[44] He wants to acquire money by transforming a spiritual gift –the "Grace" of God upon marriage– in a corporeal and sensual merchandise.

Like Felipe de Carrizales, Guzmán spends his new money in order to live like a nobleman. Idleness and gambling are, for him, the attributes of a good life; he must play with and learn how to be protected from the games of deception and expectations hidden within the apparent expressions of people. In Cervantes's *El casamiento engañoso*, the poor Ensign Campuzano attempts to become rich by marrying a lady, Estefanía, because he has seen her wearing some apparently very valuable rings. She is however just another rogue like him, ready to deceive, rob him and run. Campuzano himself confesses to his friend Peralta that the chain he was wearing did not have much worth either. Nevertheless, during the time he is married Campuzano says that: "almorzaba en la cama, levantábame a las once, comía a las doce, y a las dos sesteaba en el estrado." (Cervantes II, 286) (I had breakfast in bed, I got up at eleven, ate at twelve, and at two I took a nap in the drawing room.) In other words, he was living the life of an idle rentier.

These texts deal with the question of wealth by showing the representational status that money permits people to acquire. Works like *Guzmán de Alfarache* do not merely describe the possession or lack of material goods, but also the acquisition of a value of a different sort. Guzmán says: "Es el pobre moneda que no corre." (354) (A pauper is currency that does not circulate.) The sentence implies a conceptualization of human relations from the point of view of money, a differentiated realm of exchange and success that is at the base of the *república* of business, merchants and work.

Poor people are currency without value. It seems that Guzmán is also referring to the symbolic values that define differences in the perception and treatment of individuals, as if those values were natural attributes. The poor person:

> Come más tarde, lo peor y más caro. Su real no vale medio, su sentencia es necedad, su discreción locura, su voto escarnio, su

---

[44] In *El narrador pícaro: Guzmán de Alfarache*, Rodríguez-Matos proposes to read Guzmán's whole narration as the way that the pícaro-writer takes on different roles as a means to seduce his audience in order to obtain a benefit.

hacienda del común; ultrajado de muchos y aborrecido de todos. (*ibid.*)

(Eats later, the worst and the most expensive. His "real" [coin] is not worth half, his judgment is foolish, his discretion madness, his curse scorn, his wealth public property, outraged by many and abhorred by all.)

The poor person eats later because he must let the rich eat first; he eats the worst part, because the best is for the rich; the poor eats the most expensive food, because the poor has nothing to paid with. Therefore, nothing of what he has is worth anything: his talk is considered stupid, his capital belongs to everybody; in sum, he is injured by many and hated by everybody. An economic and cultural figure emerges from the articulation of eating badly and being rejected, and from having nothing to lacking a rational discourse. The rich man, by the contrary:

¡Qué viento en popa! ¡Con qué tranquilo mar navega! ¡Qué bonanza de cuidado! ¡Qué descuido de necesidades ajenas! [. . .] De todos es bien recibido. Sus locuras son caballerías, sus necedades sentencias. Si es malicioso, lo llaman astuto; si pródigo, liberal; si avariento, reglado y sabio; si murmurador, gracioso; si atrevido, desenvuelto; si desvergozado, alegre; si mordaz, cortesano; si incorregible, burlón; si hablador, conversable; si vicioso, afable; si tirano, poderoso [. . .] Todos le tiemblan, que ninguno se le atreve; todos cuelgan el oído de su lengua, para satisfacer a su gusto [. . .] Con lo que quiere sale. Es parte, juez y testigo. Acreditando la mentira, su poder la hace parecer verdad y, cual si lo fuese, pasan por ella [. . .] ¡Cómo lo festejan! ¡Cómo lo engrandecen! (354-5)

(What wind on the stern! On what a calm sea he sails! How care-free! How little he worries about others' necessities! [. . .] He is well received by all. His madness is a chivalrous undertaking, his foolish is judgment. If he is malicious they call him astute, if prodigal liberal, if avaricious moderate and wise, if grumbling charming, if impudent assured, if shameless happy, if mordant courtly, if incorrigible funny, if gossipy sociable, if vicious affable, if tyrannical powerful [. . .] All fear him, let no one dare him; all stand by his word, to satisfy his pleasure [. . .] He gets away with anything. He is party, judge and witness. Accrediting lies, his power makes it seem true and, as if they were, they pass for it [. . .] How they court him! How they exalt him!)

For Guzmán, to be rich is to acquire the capacity for transforming the reality of some attributes, to obtain an additional meaning in the characterization of the social projection of individuals. This transformation is possible because money introduces its evaluating mechanism even into the constitution of the body: "Porque el dinero calienta la sangre y la vivifica; y así, el que no lo tiene, es un cuerpo muerto que camina entre los vivos." (*ibid.*) (Because money warms the blood and revives it, and so, he who does not have it, is a dead body which walks among the living.)

Blood –*sangre*– refers here to the physical element of the body and also to the symbolic value of nobility. Guzmán plays with both meanings to establish the common denominator between nature and society, since, he says, the only wisdom is *tener* –to have. Guzmán considers lineage and nobility to be merely illusions that can only fulfill their pretensions through wealth. For that reason, the life of an individual must be heated –*calienta, vivifica*– by the all-powerful element that money is. Otherwise, like the Squire in *Lazarillo de Tormes*, the individual becomes a dead body wandering around in search of vital food. Guzmán goes on to say:

> Que ninguno se afrenta de tener por pariente a un rico, aunque sea vicioso, y todos huyen del virtuoso, si hiede a pobre. La riqueza es como el fuego, que, aunque asiste en lugar diferente, cuantos a él se acercan se calientan, aunque no saquen brasa, y a más fuego, más calor. (684)

> (That no one can be insulted by having a rich relative even if he is vicious, and everyone flees from the virtuous, if he stinks like a poor person. Wealth is like fire, which, even though it assists in a different place, those who approach are warmed, even if they do not take live coals, and the hotter the fire, the greater the warmth.)

The poor person stinks and the rich man, regardless of how immoral he might be, is fire, heat, the element of human survival. These and many other digressions are properly moral-economic meditations. They introduce a mercantile dimension through which the text explores a society officially subsumed within traditional notions of dependency and subordination, but which is at the same time pervaded by the reality and the perception of a competition for wealth.

We can perfectly see similar preoccupations in a letter to his friend, the reformer Pérez de Herrera, dated October 1597. Alemán reflects here on how he used to enjoy with money and expenditures the friendship of some people, who later abandoned him:

> Ya sabes mi soledad, mi flaca substancia, ya me ves por oprobio reputado. Los que de mí recibieron bien me dejaron, los que alegremente comieron a mi mesa, con rostros tristes y enfado me despiden de su puerta, negándome su conversación y compañía, que es por la ingratitud; más me duelen los que me halagaban y consolaban; querían despeñarme muchos en mi mocedad [. . .] burlé, reí, jugué [. . .] volví la cabeza, no los hallé, pasaron adelante por la posta, dejáronme atrás, y nunca más los vi. Otros volaron tan alto que se olvidaron de mí [. . .] estimábalos más que oro ni plata; faltó la plata, gastóse el oro y ellos con ello; por amigos los tuve [. . .] los granjeé con dineros. (*ibidem* 442-3)

> (You already know my solitude, my weakness, you already see me made famous by opprobrium. Those who received good by me have left, those who joyfully ate at my table, with sad countenances and anger dismiss me from their door, denying me their conversation and company, that because of ingratitude; I am hurt more by those who flattered and consoled me. Many wanted to bring me down in my youth. I joked, laughed, played [. . .] turned my head, and did not see them, they passed in front by the post, they left me behind, and I never saw them again. Others flew so high they forgot about me [. . .] I valued them more than gold or silver; the silver was gone, the gold was wasted and they with it; I had them as friends [. . .] I won them with money.)

With his own experience, Alemán relates a crisis of personal values that emerges with a wider circulation of gold and money. In the same vein that his literary work, he also points to an increasing representation of human relations by means of a sensibility that elaborates on the ideas of falsehood, deception and robbery among all. Under these conditions the question of the illegitimacy of Guzmán and its effects on his life and on his own writing acquires a clear function. Anne Cruz rightly argues that Guzmán's illegitimate origin reveals an unspecified social category that threatens the accepted definitions of hierarchy and lineage:

> Guzmán's bastard status fails to define an essential or even specific ethnic, social, or economic category. His is, instead, an overdetermined status, one that encompasses all the dubious circumstances of the "other." (Cruz 100)

Guzmán's undefined lineage is the consequence of a debt, the byproduct of the financial connection between Seville and Genoa. His father goes to Seville in order to get his share in a business deal; in the process he has sex with an old man's wife. Guzmán is born, and with him a story of the transformation of an illegitimate or negative value by means of a writing that transfigures this negative value in an irregular process of enrichment. Guzmán himself is responsible for this writing in which he annotates his credit, reputation, and material and spiritual assets.

His illegitimacy and his own person must circulate among two seemingly related conceptions of property, the feudal understanding of legitimate property according to lineage, and the emerging mercantile legitimization according to his own free valorization. Since his own self-valorization starts with a negative origin, everything appears to be artificial, the product of a fundamental and original lack and of a real beginning. Thus, Guzmán begins over and over again to make use of his negative value to increase his individual potential as well as to reflect on the way Christian precepts smoothly change to a description of the artificiality of social life. In other words, his social self is a mercantile entity to the same degree that his intellectual vision of society is grounded in the break from feudal legitimization and, then, in the capitalist ideal of a free growth.

Guzmán circulates through accounts, credits, petitions, robberies, usury, and *mohatras* (fictitious sales to increase artificially the price). His purpose is to concretize his dealings in cash, to show a growth of his self by a constant consumption of his credit, to make real his legitimacy. Guzmán's complex description of a mercantile world valorizes in monetary terms those other religious and ethnic discourses that attempted to reinforce a seigniorial hierarchy. Moreover, Juan Carlos Rodríguez considers that the implications of Guzmán's meditative discourses are to "to show the inevitability of appearances." (Rodríguez 218) I want to add that they are inevitable precisely because these appearances are elements of a world turned into a fiction and into a literature of deceptions. These appearances are mechanisms to produce a positive mark of signification and an additional value grounded in credit, in the valorization of the negative and the momentary false toward a future of actual gratification and realization of profits.

O te digo verdades o mentiras (I am telling you either truths or lies) says Guzmán to the reader, which is a concise and simple way of telling us that he is talking about a radical truth that does not leave room for discussion: take it or leave it. He is telling lies if the world actually functions according to Christian precepts; on the contrary, he is telling trues if one observes the function of fictitious values as instruments of economic increase. Guzmán shows that there is a fundamental conflict between religiously normative precepts –between what Guzmán sermonizes– and what Guzmán does, which, nevertheless, is the very justification of the need to inquiry on the self's own interests.

The conscious articulation of self-interest with politically legitimate norms emerges as the means for social advancement. At the root of a secular understanding of salvation, there seems to be a defense of the self by a reinforcement of the laws of the State and through punishment of those who break them. Guzmán informs the authorities about Soto and other galley-fellows of a pending mutiny. His companions have told him of the rebellion and ask him for advice on how to proceed; they think that above all considerations, Guzmán will be on their side against the authority that keeps them imprisoned. But Guzmán thinks otherwise: "hice mi consideración, y como siempre tuve propósito firme de no hacer cosa infame ni mala [. . .]." (*Guzmán* 904) (I made my deliberation, and [. . .] since I never wanted to do any bad action nor any infamy . . .).

Ironically, Guzmán says that since he has always intended to avoid a bad action he places himself under the king to become an informer against his galley-mates. At this final and crucial point in the writing of his life, the question is no longer to believe him or not; rather the question is to open up the transition to a personal and subjective justification for an action. He acts according to an individualized signification of freedom and economic value. This consideration is his reason to tell authority about the conspiracy. Not surprisingly, he is able to perceive at this moment the relation between his person and the legitimate form of power embedded in the State. At the juncture when his writing originates encompassing his whole life together with his drive for spiritual and material enrichment, Guzmán implies that his liberation from the galleys may parallel the salvation of his soul.

Guzmán pragmatically addresses the secular turn of the religious self that some years later Gracián will reconsider in his own version of a political morality. I argue in the next chapter that the mediating notion in this turn must be placed along a conversion of the notion of the Christian "person" for purposes of civil engagement. These civil purposes acquire in Gracián's description an intellectual emphasis as a result of a literary perspective placed upon the search for success and distinction.

Such a literary perspective reinforces the symbolic levels of the individual's assets, as well as the verbal and "political" skills of persons engaged in a process of self-improvement and self-defense. The secular turn in Gracián expresses in my view something closer to a constitution of the self by symbolic forms of wealth that reinforces the fictitious dimension of the goal-oriented sphere of human exchanges. There is properly a technical or an aesthetic level of artificiality in the world of appearances, which configures the realm of competition and success and which literature adopts as its own realm of expression.

A fictitious writing, particularly texts in the picaresque tradition, seems to explore a transition from concerns with the evaluation of the Christian soul to more pressing preoccupations with an unpredictable social life. Most literary works of the first decades of the seventeenth century intend to portray the idea that the defense of oneself depends on the proper evaluation of others' intentions. In these circumstances, individuals follow an economic intuition that often results in a vision of the civil society as a state of war.

The debates on poverty and the analyses by moral and political economists have in these decades a counterpart in the rapid publication of texts dealing with delinquency, robbery and failing attempts at social improvement. The state of war is the product of a literary sensibility that emphasizes the "anonymity" of human relations in worldly issues, particularly by depicting lives in relation to the acquisition of wealth. Several of these texts reiterate an economic definition in these human affairs, though most of the time they do it through the lens of a discourse on the threats from deceivers and social aggressors to the established order. Within this context, literature mediates the configuration of a *república* of wealth and monetary dealings, informing readers of the autonomy that the pursuit of enrichment has acquired at all levels of the seigniorial hierarchy.

In most instances, texts about the poor, the social climber, and the *pícaro* and the *pícara* in all their literary variations, depict this economic autonomy still heavily covered by the signs of an aristocratic ideology of human degradation. These characters' attempts at the satisfaction of economic goals or their search for improvement are deemed to be irregular forms of humanity, suspicious deformations of Christian norms.

In 1620 Juan de Luna gives in a *Segunda parte del Lazarillo* a dramatic picture of dispossession. There is no hope for social or economic improvement throughout his story and, much less, for any accommodation when, at the end Lázaro, badly beaten and in absolute poverty, decides to wait in a church for his death:

> Púseme en un rincón considerando los reveses de la fortuna, y que por dondequiera hay tres leguas de mal camino; y así determiné quedarme en aquella iglesia para acabar allí mi vida, que según los males pasados no podía ser muy larga, y para escusar el trabajo a los clérigos que no me fuesen a buscar a otra parte después de muerto. (Luna 387-8)
>
> (I put myself in a corner considering the reversals of fortune, and every which way there are three leagues of bad paths; and in that way I determined to stay in that church so as to end there my life, which it could not be too long because of my past sufferings, and so as to excuse the work for the clerics, that they would not look for me elsewhere after death.)

In 1620 too, Cortés de Tolosa relates in *Lazarillo de Manzanares* the story of a boy who goes from the orphanage to a family of criminals, and who at the end hopes to make a living in America. Also in 1620, Carlos García publishes in Paris his novel *La desordenada codicia de los bienes ajenos*, where from beginning to end the text takes us to a world of persistent deception and robbery. The representation of all levels of society being "possessed" by thieves acquires a dark satirical twist that seems to point to the belief that the world surrendered to sin. Moreover, this seventeenth-century sin expresses an insatiable search for somebody else's wealth:

> De aquí infiero el engaño notable en que vive hoy el mundo, creyendo que la pobreza fue inventora del hurto, no siendo otro que la riqueza y prosperidad; porque el amor y deseo de la honra crece, cuando ella mesma se aumenta [. . .] De aquí entenderá vuestra merced que el hurtar es naturaleza en el hombre y no artificio, y que va por herencia y propagación en todo el linaje humano. (García 73)

> (From here I infer the notable deception in which the world lives today, believing that poverty was the inventor of robbery when, on the contrary, it was wealth and prosperity: because the love and the wish for honor grows when that itself grows. Thus, you may understand that robbery is in the nature of man and not something acquired, and that it goes by heritage through all of humankind.)

This depiction of a defective human nature seems to reinforce the vision of a fallen man, but along very particular secular traits in the way the continuation of sin points to enrichment and deviant attitudes encouraged by it. According to this vision, a defective nature inherently nurtured in the social milieu explains the proliferation of dangers and social violence against certain people. The narrative frame of the collection *Guía y aviso de forasteros que vienen a esta corte*, published in 1620 by Liñán y Verdugo, involves two friends in Madrid, "el uno pleiteante y el otro pretendiente" (one was a plaintiff, the other was a public office-seeker) who, at the Palace's door, meet a man that has just arrived from a province to resolve a problem with an inheritance. The friends advise the newcomer on the dangers that he will face in the city-court. The first advice is to find a good inn:

> de gente que viva bien, y en buena vecindad, que sea en calle de barrio, y población honrada: de lo cual suele ser indicativo el estar adornada de casas y edificios altos, ricos y bien labrados, donde de ordinario vive gente noble y principal, rica y poderosa. (Liñán y Verdugo 61-62)

> (of people who live well, and in good company, that it be in the street of a barrio, and honorable population; the indicators of which tend to be that it is adorned with houses and high buildings, rich and well bricked, where noble, rich and powerful normally live.)

An unmistakable expression of class awareness, they indicate that the best way to avoid criminals, thieves and poor people is by staying in the wealthy areas of the city. Most of the stories follow the same pattern: *pícaros* and *pícaras* ready to plot an attack against imprudent men.

In spite of the aristocratic fictionalization of the new social relations, these texts show the working of a different set of ideas in human business. While the topics of a deceitful humanity and a corrupted materiality –particularly the materiality of sex– reinforce the Christian-medieval discourse on a degraded world, they also express unknown conditions regarding the expectations and goals for a mobile population. The emphasis on deception during the crisis of the early modernity re-situates, in Resina's analysis, the place of trust within the expectations of the social actors:

> What is new is not the need for trust but the systematization of contingency that makes trust socially necessary and thus its potential disappointment as well. ("Cervantes's Confidence Games..." 241)

The increasing autonomy of the still-marginal society of private business reaches the fiction of literature precisely stressing the major role that the ghostly appearance of money and monetary dealings has in the fabric of individual hopes, fears and distrusts. The literature of the *república* –the fictitious writing of the emerging civil society– attempts at exhausting the relations between reality and fiction to such a degree never imagined by the writing of the aristocratic mind –that is, essentially, the pastoril and the chivalric tales.

Francisco Rico saw in *Lazarillo de Tormes* the beginning of the impulse to bring the categories of literature close to the categories of "reality," that is to the historical time of human beings.[45] This impulse flourishes in the very realm of fiction, converting deception and falsehood in "one of the major thematic considerations" of the reading of literature.[46] I would even say that this literature becomes the mediation of a complex conversation between reality and fiction that ambitions to fully expand the connections between the

---

[45] *Lazarillo de Tormes* is "la exploración de la realidad cotidiana bajo la especie de ficción," (the investigation of everyday life through fiction) affirmed Rico (166).
[46] See Ife, 172.

mind, the self, and the external world. The literature of the *república* mediates Don Quijote and his world, in the first place because *Don Quijote* is a book of entertainment both in reality and in fiction; but also, because the expectations of Alonso Quijano about himself and the world are contradictorily realized through the fiction of don Quijote. In this sense, don Alonso is not less –nor more– real than, for example, Estebanillo González, the character of the 1646 picaresque novel that could have been very well written by a historical Estebanillo.[47]

The beginning of a representation of the autonomy of the economic life coincides with the disengagement of the fictitious writing of the *república* from the constraints of the aristocratic courtly lover and the legendary travels of the knight. In clear distinction to the legendary knight and the literary don Quijote, Estebanillo travels throughout the war of the empire and allied kingdoms, changing nations, armies and occupations. He becomes a mercenary, then abandons the battle-field; he spends a good deal of his time in the taverns and bears the jeering and maltreatment of the powerful people, hoping that one of them will finally protect him. The fragile humanity of Estebanillo reflects the conditions of a life that has become independent of the seigniorial values. His marginal status reflects both the aristocratic view of the promising of order and salvation only through a strict hierarchy of seigniorial power, and the early bourgeois conviction of the moral superiority of self-accomplishment.

This conviction is born in the soul of the person in spite of lineage, or rather –as Lázaro de Tormes convincingly wrote– in opposition to it and as its negation.

---

[47] Spadaccini and Zahareas's Introduction to their critical edition to *Estebanillo* studies this issue in detail.

Chapter 2

A BOURGEOIS SELF. THE CHRISTIAN PERSON
IN THE WORLD

In the following pages, I shall argue that the term "person" acquires an additional meaning, beyond the medieval and scholastic position. Since the theological controversies on the Trinity and particularly within Thomist philosophy, the person was a metaphysical term intended to define the material and divine attributes of the human being. In that sense, the person was the dignity of "individuals" who possess reason and will and, above all other entities (such as animals), were endowed (by God) with self-determination.

A new emphasis on the person begins with an effort to recuperate ideas of Christian virtue to serve the social projection of reformers and writers disengaged from the culture of rentism. It becomes a feature of a new literary space that provides an instrument to reflect on the intellectual development of the *república* from the private space of an individual reading.

Social validation of the self becomes an agonistic endeavor, a search for a community of educated men that would confront the values of unproductive consumption and the hypocritical spirituality of aristocratic classes. It can be argued that *Lazarillo de Tormes* initiates a literary evaluation of human beings according to the degree of their commitment to the pursuit of a goodness that lies in growth and in the capacity to assess the evils and errors of social interaction. The growth of the self and the widening of social expectations in Lázaro and Mateo Alemán's *pícaro*, Guzmán, are economic tendencies within the representation of a new space of inner reflection and morality.

From the anonymous publication of *Lazarillo* in 1554 to 1637-1651, the years when Gracián publishes his major texts under a pseudonym, a bourgeois-Christian "person" emerges within the context of the decapitalization of Castile, the victory of the Church over Reform and the increasing, though crippled, imperialist policy of the Monarchy.

While religious tolerance and diversity is still a creative force in the intellectual background of *Lazarillo*, the Catholic Church reigns over the struggles of the seventeenth century reasserting the Habsburg's power in Europe, a dynasty by necessity more inclined to forcefully adopt the Roman doctrines of spiritual obedience. The religious dimension of the person, thus, suffers the influences of these convulsions but maintains a social and cultural relevance in literary representations.

We obviously cannot find in Gracián the anti-clerical determination of Lázaro's narrative or his satirical use of biblical references. On the other hand, Lázaro's insights on hypocrisy are naive and childish if we compare them with Gracián's description of a general, irreparable and evil stupidity. Yet, both share the feeling that the Christian person must impose itself on society to articulate a norm of conduct for the enrichment of the best people.

The author of *Lazarillo* elaborates on the intellectual commitment of the humanist writer with the economic and moral dimensions of life in lower classes. In Alemán's *Guzmán de Alfarache* the person acquires a clear and dramatic economic definition, while in Gracián the person is the finest accomplishment of a life-long struggle to confront the conditions that threaten his privileged status.

The reconsideration of the person's virtues takes place within an emergent discrimination of spheres of social activity, which ultimately would imply the description of a necessary area of private, individual and secular profits. The person in *Lazarillo de Tormes* and *Guzmán de Alfarache* benefits from the assertion that one's own life must and can be understood through a representation of its projection into the productive sphere, that is a projection into the transactions expressing an economic value.

There is nothing in *Lazarillo* to suggest that the Christian idea is not present. On the contrary, the idea of self-determination acquires with Lázaro de Tormes a paradigmatic turn, although it does not refer exclusively to the higher dialogue with the divine essence proposed by Thomism. It rather indicates the will to transform himself and grow out of certain conditions. For that reason, Lázaro's person has a higher value than members of the nobility.

However, the major change in the person seems to be in the very notion of Lázaro's "life." It is with the idea of *mi persona* (my person) that Lázaro opens the space of intimacy, privacy and individuality. Lázaro's person belongs to his own life, in distinction to any other life of any other person. His person is his own property amid many persons and not merely a qualification for a higher individual entity in the abstract.

This personhood is the attribute of the life of an individual. This is an attribute that the "yo" (the self) possesses (*mi* persona) and that Lázaro feels impelled to disclose by his writing. In doing so, Lázaro's person is on his way to individuality and self-consciousness and, though those more contemporary terms will acquire full expression with the outcome of the bourgeois state, they configure the intellectual horizon in which Lázaro's story acquires full complexity.

For his part, the notion of the person in Gracián signals another change in the Christian idea. Gracián's person deepens the attribute of self-determination and, like Lázaro's, it is the term to discriminate among human beings rather than among individual entities in the Thomist sense. However, Gracián describes his person as a goal to be attained by selected individuals. These individuals reach, then, a higher differentiation from the rest of society or the *vulgo* (populace). Moreover, Lázaro's own life –his private person– has been modified to eradicate any symptom of acquiescence with lower classes; on the contrary, Gracián's person is an attribute of the cultured groups and shows an unmistakable consciousness of distinction.

From the story of *Lazarillo* to Gracián, the person constitutes the subject of individually-oriented decisions and exchanges, either as purely economic decisions or as symbolic values. Picaresque texts, in particular, disclose a world of poverty behind those decisions. Juan Carlos Rodríguez has argued that this literature of the "poor" functioned as the ideological matrix of a bourgeois thought. In his view, the poor individual represents the figure of a dispossessed soul that shows itself as a self-created entity. This literary character confronted the "substantialist" ideology of feudal classes, in which there is no self but the self of a blood, a lineage, a heritage, a House.

The poor individual is an empty being who claims for himself only his own life, the happenings of somebody who had never a history:

> Sin vida propia no hay narración picaresca, pero sin narración picaresca no hay vida propia. La vida sólo se produce, sólo existe, en el relato. La literatura y la vida comienzan a "vivirse juntas" precisamente a través de una vida que nunca había tenido vida: la vida de un pobre, el mayor de los pobres, el que ha aprendido a vivir a ciegas. (Rodríguez 194)

> (There is no picaresque narration without one's own life, but one's own life does not exist without picaresque narration. Life is only produced, it exists only in the story. Literature and life begin 'to be lived together' precisely through a life that had never had life: a poor man's life, the poorest, the one who has learnt to live blindly.)

Lázaro's voice, according to Rodríguez, enunciates the principle of privacy on which the bourgeoisie founded new social relations. He does so by presenting himself as a subject worthy of publication and emergence into the public sphere:

> el animismo "ve" el espacio público como algo efectivamente dominado por el "honor" –por los valores nobiliarios– y por eso se retira a lo privado. Para el organicismo, en cambio –que no "ve" el espacio público–, el hecho de que sus valores reinen en ese espacio sólo implica que reinan en el "Mundo". (Rodríguez 155)

> (animism 'sees' public space as something dominated by 'honor' –by the values of the nobility– and because of that it retreats to the private. However, for organicism –that does not 'see' the public space–, the fact that its values rule in this space only implies that they rule in the 'World.')

The feudal class does not see a distinction between its public projection and its identity as a class, further conflating its values with the values of a 'substantial' reality. This is the reason that a nobleman, according to Rodríguez, does not publish his privacy, since there is no identity beyond his public definition, there is nothing beyond the being of a lineage and of a blood.

It is only when the bourgeoisie recognizes its own identity as a class centered on a private sphere, that the *yo* –the I– has a voice in itself:

> Sólo para los lázaros (para las clases inferiores en general) se abría, pues, la posibilidad de entregar su vida "privada" al pasto

> y al juicio del público. O más estrictamente: sólo para el nombre de un pobre –sólo bajo el nombre de un pobre– podía mostrarse públicamente a sí misma, mostrar su auténtico objeto (y raíz) ideológico: el "yo", el alma privada. (Rodríguez 116)

> (Then, the possibility to present their 'private' lives to the public field and judgment was only available to the "lázaros" [for the inferior classes in general]. More precisely: only for the name of a poor person –only under the name of a poor person– they could publicly show themselves, their authentic ideological object (and root): the 'I', the private soul.)

Only a beggar offered an excuse for the rising bourgeois ideology –the *animismo*– to condense in writing an individual's private life and, most importantly, a justification to publish a self to the public. Rodríguez, thus, seems to establish a relationship between the new ideology of a "private soul" and the reality of poverty, a relationship born in contradiction as the new social relations develop into a capitalist society.

The bourgeois individual speaks with the beggar's voice and takes his dispossession as being the story of the bourgeois's soul: "El 'yo' del Lazarillo es el 'alma' del animismo necesitada básicamente del 'diálogo', de la 'relación', para expresarse, para subsistir." (Rodríguez 128) (The 'I' of Lazarillo is the 'soul' of animism in need basically of 'dialogue', of 'relation,' in order to express itself and to survive.)

The relational characteristic of this voice –the dialogue in the picaresque– brings forward the conflictive nature of this ideological matrix. It intends to represent the anti-aristocratic position of the bourgeoisie through a life that is a symptom of new social relations breaking through the old order.

Lázaro begins his story with his origins in order to offer, he says, a complete picture of his person. He writes a complete account to justify his involvement in the *caso*, to translate a particular issue into a general description of the conditions of that case. For, regardless of the correct understanding of the case –whether it refers to himself consenting his wife's adultery, or rather it points to the Archpriest's improper sexual or economic conduct–, Lázaro wants to communicate his life.

Juan Carlos Rodríguez rightly argues that with *Lazarillo* the narration of one's own life emerges at the moment that a life becomes one's own object:

> A partir del *Lazarillo*, el relato picaresco se estructura como la materialización misma de la cronología. Contar una 'vida propia' es un hecho inseparable de la aparición de la 'vida' como objeto propio, como algo delimitado estrictamente entre el nacer y el morir. (Rodríguez 139)

> (Beginning with *Lazarillo*, the picaresque story is structured as the materialization of chronology itself. Telling 'one's own life' is an event inseparable from the emergence of 'life' as one's own object, as something strictly limited between birth and death.)

I believe that death is not such a crucial element since the *pícaro* himself *writes* his life. Lázaro has so far defeated death with his cunning intelligence and his economic struggles. Nevertheless, Rodríguez is right in the sense that Lázaro's life is, beyond question, his own life and therefore it is a life that has an origin.

Lazarillo's origins become important factors to evaluate his present. He contends that his origins are an essential component of his person and his person, in turn, an inseparable articulation of events.

> Y pues Vuestra Merced escribe se le escriba y relate el caso muy por extenso, parecióme no tomalle por el medio sino del principio porque se tenga entera noticia de mi persona, y también porque consideren los que heredaron nobles estados cuán poco se les debe, pues fortuna fue con ellos parcial, y cuánto más hicieron los que, siéndoles contraria con fuerza y maña remando salieron a buen puerto. (*Lazarillo* 95-7)

> (And since Your Grace writes asking that I write and relate the case to you extensively, I did not want to take it from the middle but from the beginning so you can have the whole picture about my person; also so that those who inherited noble status may consider how little is owed to them because fortune sided with them, and those with an ill fortune can sense how much more they did with strength and dexterity rowing to arrive at a safe harbor.)

A complete account of his person seems to be a novelty and a distinguished "thing" which deserves to be communicated: "Yo por bien tengo que cosas tan señaladas, y por ventura nunca oídas ni vistas, vengan a noticia de muchos..." (91) (I take it as something good that such outstanding things, never heard or seen before, become news known by many...).

Lázaro complements the case he was told to write about with information on an important thing (*cosa*), which happens to be his person. He is going to write about his person and, thus, he establishes the paradigmatic split between himself as narrator, and his own person as the object of his writing. In other words, Lázaro transforms the possible questions of sexual impropriety or simony into the question about himself. He is the *noticia* that deserves to be known, his person is the *cosa tan señalada*.

The uniqueness of Lazarillo is the object of his writing. Moreover, there is a major relationship between the uniqueness of his person and the value of an economic change in the life of an individual. Lázaro becomes the voice of himself in regard to the radical singularity that his person represents. This singularity is the foundation on which the individual economic change lays, making any other qualification –such as heritage– a lesser novelty, a thing already known.

The value placed on economic change determines the structure of the intellectual engagement of some Christian writers with the poor areas of Spanish, particularly Castilian, society. This engagement becomes a new discourse of its own and contributes to the formation of the emergent civil society where individuals struggle out of economic needs and for a valorization of the economic change in itself.

This positive evaluation of change in the economic arena manifests, however, a contradictory evolution during the period that the present study covers. As I showed in the previous chapter, economic considerations exploded into writing as the debates on poverty and currency reached an intellectual and a political dimension in the *república*. The seigniorial groups tended to react negatively to the slow but steady opening of mercantile spaces, to the point that during the stagnation of the first two decades of the seventeenth century mercantile activities will be degraded in a manner comparable to the reinforcement of aristocratic values such as honor and *sangre*.

The major vehicle for the transmission of these ideas is the theater, the *comedia*, where the seigniorial hierarchy reinforces a system of privileges by displacing individual as well as collective conflicts into an ideal participation of all classes in those aristocratic values.[1] The literature of the *república* too suffers the intrusion of the aristocratic ideology, particularly in the representation of individual drives. The road from *Lazarillo* to the literature on *pícaros*, as I pointed out before and I will emphasize later on, is a paradigmatic example of the increasing imposition of an aristocratic perspective on the impulses for a free "person" of the bourgeois mind.

Within the seigniorial perspective, novelty and change are threatening aspects of unrestricted human exchanges. Analyzing the transformations that led to the end of the Renaissance in Europe at large, Bouwsma has recently stated:

> The period continued to be deeply aware of the importance of time and change. But change was also increasingly perceived as dangerous; it was therefore another source of anxiety in an anxious age. Thus, while it was studied by some and even celebrated, the awareness of change also stimulated resistance and denial. By the later sixteenth century, history, which has usually been understood as an account of times past and therefore of change, was languishing, put to partisan and polemical purposes, or being replaced by mythical claims that supported one or another special interest. (Bouwsma 199)

This reaction against change is one of the major cultural features that Maravall has put forward in his characterization of the "conservative" turn that the second half of the sixteenth century witnessed in Spain, which will determine dramatically the "crisis" of the Baroque. Picaresque literature receives vehemently the contradictions involved in the ideas of change and transformation, and their impact on individuals and the social order. Among the changes

---

[1] Maravall's analysis of the ideological function of theater in the Baroque is, in my view, very convincing, particularly in terms of the role of the *comedia* in the fictionalization and promotion of integrative values for all classes; see his *Teatro y literatura en el siglo XVII*. The popular and entertaining character of theater contributed to the reinforcement of a feeling of identification and participation from the part of the people with the seigniorial structure of power routinely staged in the *comedia*. In *La cultura del Barroco*, Maravall developed his sociological interpretation of Baroque theater within the context of a political reaction of the landed aristocracy. Cohen, on the other hand, gives a brilliant comprehensive (and comparative) interpretation of theater that emphasizes an ideological struggle between dominant and contesting forces in *Drama of a Nation*. Whether one reads the *comedia* as an ideological machine or as a field of struggle, the fact remains that it created a familiar and obsessive pattern for the representation of the seigniorial and monarchical power.

that the literature will reflect or combat, we can easily find the "aspiration to move upward":

> La estimación positiva de la pretensión de elevarse, de subir a más, de medrar, por parte de aquel que se ve estamentalmente reducido a un bajo nivel, empieza a difundirse y a representar, en mi entender, una de las más serias alteraciones de la moral social –y no menos de la moral del individuo– en los siglos modernos. (Maravall, *La literatura picaresca* 358)

> (The positive consideration of the pretense to move upwards –to jump up socially, to *medrar*– by those who are reduced to a lower level by the system of estates, begins to spread out, and in my opinion it represents one of the most serious alterations of the social morality –and not less of the individual morality– within the modern centuries.)

In other words, the conditions for individual disengagement from the seigniorial structure become more acute along those new expectations and spaces that strive for a free and an unrestricted human exchange. The positive evaluation of this novelty in the words of some characters, like Lázaro de Tormes, must confront later on the intense and adverse judgment made upon them, particularly by the narrators of most of the literature of *pícaros*.

Lazarillo de Tormes, thus, is the first text where a recounting of somebody's life becomes a defense of a *person* in the world, that is an affirmation of its intrinsic value in front of any authority or aristocratic status. Moreover, Lázaro carries on this defense through his writing, both fictitiously within the letter to Vuestra Merced, and effectively in the text of a book, which becomes, with many others after it, a cultural product of the *república*:

The triangular situation at the end of this letter-book, the relation between Lázaro's wife and the Archpriest, is the case that Lázaro effaces by bringing forward the "negative" case of a nobody's life (Rodríguez 193). This life, however, is the life of a *person*. The story about himself introduces the Christian person as a cultural field of an emergent bourgeois writing contesting –in the case of *Lazarillo de Tormes*– the Church.

In the scholastic tradition, the person became the notion that intended to define the participation or belonging of individual human beings to the Christian doctrine. The purpose was to differentiate human beings from any other being, that is from exclusively rational beings (angelical beings) on the one hand, and from non-rational beings, on the other. The person would occupy a middle ground in which its individuality (its materiality, so to speak) was only one aspect of its being. The other aspects were its reason and its will (its self-determination) which signaled a participation in God.[2]

For our purposes, it is important to take note of the appropriation that Lázaro realizes of this notion in order to signify the subject of his life, thus introducing with his own person the institutional sphere of the Church. In other words, the Church and its discourses on the person are the implicit intellectual world upon which the narration of Lázaro's life unfolds.

By articulating his life from the beginning, Lázaro seems also to establish a particular approach to one of the debates in which the Church is involved, the debate on poverty. He explicitly states that his life is valuable in terms of the economic change it represents, above and beyond the economic welfare of the nobility, for which the origins of the individual are supposed to reach further back before birth. The lineage of the nobleman does not correspond to the historical time of a single life; on the contrary, the very idea of lineage consists of the legitimization of privileges that transcend the historical time of individual beings.

Lázaro reflects on the economic change of a person by narrating his disengagement from the cultural and social space of Church. The space where he acquires a value is the emergent space of economic dealings where the person engages in transactions in order to pursue his own interest. Lázaro's person rises, then, at the intersection created by the breaking down of a *universal* discourse of legitimization of a Christian society. In other words, Lázaro's person confronts the ecclesiastical institution by expressing a Christian engagement with the economic change that conform the roots of the bourgeois society, which Ortiz and other contemporaries call the *república*.

The biblical references and the ironic contempt for ecclesiastical people place Lazarillo's life in a demonstration of intellectual force against the hypocrisy of the members of the Church. This

---

[2] See Maritain, *The Person and the Common Good*, p. 23 and Norris Clark, *Person and Being*, p. 27, both commenting on the Thomist legacy.

moral attack unveils a literary space negatively structured against the institutional discourses that attempted to preserve the universality of the Church. Whatever feelings readers have toward Lázaro, the fact remains that his life is always of a higher value than those of the Maqueda's priest, Merced's frier, Bull's dispenser or the Archpriest of San Salvador.

These Church's workers are responsible for Lázaro's experiences and ideas in so far as they represent vicious behavior with multiple consequences in the moral and social teaching of the Christians. These people are close to lower classes and are supposed to transmit the Christian doctrine to those people. Lázaro constructs the story of his person through several episodes having in common —most of them at least— the description of a moral defect in the conduct of Christians.

Lázaro's life opens a literary space that reveals a transformation in the conception of the person. While the Christian idea of the transcendent quality of the person maintains its force, its historical subjection lies outside the *dominium* of the Church. The anonymous writer puts forward a notion of the person self-constituted by his own value –by his own life. This self-constitution receives a practical orientation the moment the person embodies the economic needs of the bourgeoisie: the freedom of the self to engage in transactions and exchanges that may benefit his aspirations.

Authenticity means, for Lázaro, to be truthful to himself. This is the reason that the Squire is such a pitiful figure, since his hypocrisy is not but the individual extreme of a social disease. This is the disease of the subjugation of people to the demands of cultural discourses or values that refer, directly or indirectly, to the *de facto* alliance between the *rentier* classes and the Church. Lázaro considers authenticity to be the definition of persons who have broken through that alliance, resulting in the possibility of a new culture.

This new culture cannot be the one represented by the people of the Church that Lazarillo meets. He stands in isolation from those people, in a relationship of internal confrontation. He presents himself by showing the way he disengages from them, and by the force of a superior morality that acquires full explanation in the particular relationship the narrator establishes with his own person.

The injunction against nobility from the point of view of an early bourgeois discourse rests on the very same prologue: "porque consideren los que heredaron nobles estados, cuán poco se les debe..." (so the ones who inherited noble states may consider how little is owed to them). We need to ask for the subject behind the impersonal construction: who is the one not owing much to the nobility? Or, in other words, who can discriminate about the proper rewards due to different people? I think the answer refers directly to an emergent subject of a "national" wealth.

The reason for this injunction is further explained by means of the exemplary bourgeois ideology of the *tabula rasa*: "pues Fortuna fue con ellos parcial." (because Fortune sided with them). A biased fate has given wealth to the nobility, but has not given them the value that comes with work: "y cuánto más hicieron los que, siéndoles contraria..." (and those with a contrary Fortune, how much more they did). The value of self-improvement is, we may conclude, the value that must be rewarded, the value that really pertains to a new subject that is, above all, concerned with the fate of the society as opposed to the destinies of particular Houses.

This impersonal subject, capable of discriminating and distributing rewards, must not be other than a new society ruled by a proper government. Without going that far, Lázaro shifts the direction of his indictment against a worthless nobility to a yet undefined axis of integration of work and wealth. This impersonal subject recreates a point of view that Lázaro somehow shares even though it goes beyond his own perspective. This is the point of view that illuminates the space of the larger debates through which a distinct sphere of civil relations and exchanges begins to surface as the home of the bourgeoisie.

Lázaro's voice articulates the bourgeois need to construct that home. His voice fuses the elements of the social classes that would benefit the most from the emergence of a system of merits and unrestricted mobility of people, as well as from the substitution of an ethics of personal authenticity for the practices of the Church.

The home of the bourgeoisie comprises both the home of an ideal married couple and the neighboring areas of enrichment. Both will be seen by the bourgeois man as spaces of virtue and means to self-realization. Lázaro's marriage is one of convenience, we know, and one that degrades him to a certain extent; but it is a marriage that also shows the subordination that virtuous persons suffer in the face of material needs and corrupted people of the Church. In this regard it is revealing the fact that in certain moral considerations made by political economists and in several instances of Mateo Alemán's *Guzmán de Alfarache*, the question of marriage acquires an even greater value when it is seen in the light of the question of wealth.

The literature of the *república* at the end of the sixteenth century shows an important and revealing paradox in Mateo Alemán's *Guzmán de Alfarache*. On the one hand, the representation of economic needs becomes explicitly articulated in the full development of an irregular and frustrated project of enrichment; on the other hand, the seigniorial attempt to degrade and devalue mercantile activities within the context of an increasing volatility of the currency, determines the reinforcement of the subordination of the individual drives (represented by the *pícaros*). This subordination takes the form of a clear ideological alliance between so-called orthodox norms of the Church and aristocratic principles.

Alemán, however, manages to produce a novelistic figure that expresses more than any other this paradox, while maintaining the bourgeois initiative for an assertive and secular person. As Francisco Rico saw:

> En nuestra novela [*Guzmán*], las realidades aludidas y las maneras de aludirlas carecen de sentido mientras no se refieran a Guzmán, mientras no se advierte que son *cosas que le pasan* a Guzmán. La esencia del libro, así, no es tanto mostrarnos las cosas, como presentarnos a Guzmán percibiéndolas e incorporándoselas. (Rico 97-98)
>
> (In our novel, alluded realities and the way to allude them do not make sense if they are not referred to Guzmán, if we do not observe that they are *things that happen to Guzmán*. The essence of the book, thus, is not to show things, but rather to represent Guzmán perceiving them and assuming them to him.)

This subjectivity is the result of Guzmán's interest in writing his life as an example of the way the world works; that is, as an example of the contradictions in the search for wealth. Clearly, Alemán writes the story of a *pícaro* who wants to be rich. Guzmán, unlike Lazarillo, always has the acquisition of wealth in mind and, unlike Lazarillo, has experienced since his childhood moments of scarcity, poverty and well being. In other words, *Guzmán de Alfarache* does not represent the life of someone escaping poverty, but rather the life of a problematic enrichment.

This is a process that, in Cavillac's analysis, reflects the ethical and economic concerns of the Castilian bourgeoisie:

> Inspirado por la imperfecta burguesía que los mecanismos monetarios instauraban en Castilla, ese moralismo puritano, obra de 'letrados' a menudo emparentados con comerciantes, alimenta de hecho una reflexión sobre la esencia del *capitalismo* destinada a liberar al mercader de su pecado original de usura que la especulación financiera fomentaba mediante el veneno del crédito, paralizando así su libre albedrío. Paralelamente, esa impostura de un crédito ficticio se veía objetivada en el traficante traidor a la *mercancía*, el mendigo ducho en explotar la caridad y el noble ocioso encastillado en el mito de su superioridad. A través del parasitismo de estos tres tipos sociales se hallaba condenada toda una axiología aristocrática basada en el *otium cum dignitate*.
>
> Este reformismo burgués latente va a cuajar, en torno a 1600, en un programa político de restauración nacional cuya clave debía ser el "retorno a la mercancía". (Cavillac 597)

> (Inspired by the imperfect bourgeoisie installed in Castile by monetary mechanisms, this puritan morality –a product of "letrados" often related to merchants– in fact made possible a reflection of the essence of *capitalism* that could free the merchant of his original sin of usury that financial speculation fostered with the poison of credit, and that paralyzed his free will. At the same time, the fraud of fictitious credit was concretized in the dealer-traitor to the *merchandise*, the expert beggar who exploited charity and the idle nobleman enclosed in the myth of superiority. By and through the parasitism of these three social types a whole aristocratic axiology based on the *otium cum dignitate* was condemned.
>
> This latent bourgeois reformism would crystallize around 1600 in a political program of national restoration whose key was something like the "return to the merchandise.")

In order to overcome his degraded and sinful soul, the *pícaro* Guzmán must convert to a purified ethics of work and social responsibility. His degradation has been the result of economic idleness and a lack of participation in the common good. Along this conversion Guzmán exposes the moral evils of a corrupted enrichment:

> Mediante la sacralización de la noción de intercambio, centrada en la idea de que 'ninguno puede hacerse rico de ajena sustancia', sino que debe prosperar por su labor ya que 'al bien ocupado no hay virtud que le falte', el *Guzmán de Alfarache* plantea las bases de una ética puritana en la que van parejas regeneración espiritual y renovación social. Este voluntarismo perfectista, que identifica el Bien con la ley del trabajo fecundo, apela en definitiva a una dignificación del burgués, fermento de una sociedad en la que el dinero, en vez de fijar el poder, lo redistribuiría vitalizando así la colectividad de los *Hombres Nuevos*. (Cavillac 536)

> (By the blessing of the notion of exchange –centered around the idea that 'nobody can become rich from somebody else's substance,' but must prosper by his work since 'there is no missing virtue in the one who is well employed'– *Guzmán de Alfarache* establishes the basis of a puritan ethics in which spiritual regeneration and social restoration go together. This rigorous will that identifies the Good with the law of fruitful work, calls in sum for giving dignity to the bourgeois, the ferment of a society where money, rather than making of power something fixed, would redistribute it energizing the collectivity of the *New Men*.)

The moral dimension of his story is an aspect of his economic digressions on the failure of a merchant in a civil society corrupted by the lack of virtue and the madness of "aristocratization." His desire to live as a rentier and the financial wrongdoings by which he intends to acquire wealth are the social and psychological traits of a culture pervaded by the habits of an unproductive consumption. The lack of virtue in his economic behavior, particularly in his behavior as a dealer or a merchant, is also reflected in his experiences with women and marriage.

The virtuous marriage will become one of the core issues in the development of privacy within the bourgeois subject. It is within the private sphere that the Christian couple is supposed to create the conditions for the enrichment of their soul. This enrichment must ground the economic activity of a man who thus becomes a man of business. González de Cellorigo, as many other political economists, sees the relationship in "civil life" between the creation of wealth and an increase of the population. Men, he says, do not want to marry because they do not properly esteem women and because women are very "expensive":

> la tierra es muy aparejada para producir cuanto conviene a la vida civil y a sustentar más de lo que sustenta. A lo cual no es de poco estorbo estar las mujeres de España en tan poca estimación de los hombres, que huyendo del matrimonio desamparan la procreación y dan en extremos viciosos. [. . .] Procede también esto porque las mujeres son gravemente costosas según el estado presente [. . .] y doncellas muy virtuosas, por faltarles las dotes, se están arrinconadas. (González de Cellorigo 58)
>
> (the earth is too well suited for producing as much as is convenient for civil life and for sustaining more than what it sustains. Thus, it is no small bother that men in Spain esteem women so little, fleeing from wedlock they forsake procreation and take to extreme vices. [. . .] This also occurs because women are terribly expensive at the present time [. . .] and very virtuous maidens, lacking dowries, are neglected.)

Guzmán's actions in relation to both marriage and enrichment are wrong, in the sense that they do not constitute a virtuous union and a productive activity. In Madrid he becomes a merchant with the money and jewelry he has stolen in Italy, and marries the daughter of another corrupt merchant with the idea of increasing their mutual capital. The following description of Guzmán's bankruptcy shows us the combination of fraudulent loans together with his wife's extreme expenditures in luxury. The economic reflection points out to the vicious circle of financial wrongdoing and women's unproductive expenditure.

These moral and economic reflections are motivated by the need of the emergent bourgeoisie to legitimize a mercantile society through a Christian household devoted to economic sobriety. In several other episodes Guzmán depicts women as the cause of his problems. We find the same pattern also in many other picaresque novels and short stories, where female rogues –the *pícaras*– transform marriage and sexual seduction in instruments of economic aggression.[3] Maravall has indicated that this trend reinforced a traditional and chauvinist mentality aimed at blocking the social mobility of women:

---

[3] See Peter Dunn, *Spanish Picaresque Fiction*, pp. 232-251, for a critical account of the stories with female rogues.

> la carga de mantener a rajatabla el honor conyugal y familiar va ligada, entiendo yo, en el siglo XVII especialmente, a cuestiones de paternidad y propiedad, pero no únicamente, sino también a todo el régimen de organización y transmisión del dominio en la sociedad. (Maravall, *La literatura picaresca* 643)

> (In the 17th century I think that the goal of maintaining rigorously the conjugal and familial honor is not only linked to questions of paternity and property, but also to the whole regime of the organization and transmission of domination in society.)

The representation of marriage in these terms permits one to argue that a domestic space becomes a matter of concern for the economic projection of the bourgeois person. The marriage of a merchant must result in a productive articulation of spheres that defines the self as a proprietor: "presumía de que mi casa, mi mujer y mi persona siempre anduviésemos bien tratados y en mi negociación ser un reloj." (Alemán 767) (I took care that my house, my wife and my person were always well treated, and to be timely in my business.)

We may notice the value of punctuality in relation to his mercantile and financial deals, and the close relation between his good timing in business and the well being of his property. Since he includes his physical and bodily materiality, Guzmán seems to express by "my person" an intimate awareness of himself that identifies his actions and his words.

However, Guzmán's marriage and business are corrupt because they respond to an unproductive consumption, an economic behavior that degrades the domestic space and leads to failure in the bourgeois society. When the time of payments comes, he does not have the money he has fictitiously accumulated in false loans. Guzmán, then, bitterly complains about the whole spectrum of fraudulent loans and he proposes to eradicate them from Castile. Moreover, he expressly mentions his person as involved in the economic process and as the bearer of the legal and financial consequences. The person receives and is responsible for the credit and expenditures:

> Para engañar con su persona, si quiere tratar de casarse con mucha dote, hace lo mismo: busca haciendas en confianza y como después de casado crecen las obligaciones y no pueden

con el gasto, cobra lo suyo su dueño y quedan los desposados padeciendo necesidad. Luego, conocido el engaño, falta el amor y algunas y aun muchas veces llegan a las manos, porque la mujer no consiente que se venda su hacienda o no quiere obligarse a las deudas del marido. (Alemán 773)

(In order to deceive with his person, if he wants to marry with much dowry he does the same: he looks for property in trust, and since after being married debts grow and they cannot bear all expenses the owner cashes in his part and the couple is left in need. Later, when they find the fraud, love disappears, and many times they fight because the woman does not permit her property to be sold or does not want to share her husband's debts.)

We must notice again the relation between fraudulent loans and a vicious marriage. Guzmán becomes the voice of the reformer, as Cavillac demonstrated, and directly participates in the construction of a subject of wealth of a quasi-national projection:

Y en Castilla, donde se contrata la máquina del mundo sin hacienda, sin fianzas ni abonos, más de con solo buena maña para saber engañar a los que se fían dellos, toman tratos para que sería necesario en otras partes mucho caudal con que comenzarlos y muy mayor para el puesto que ponen. (Alemán 771-2)

(And in Castile, where the machine of the world is engaged without wealth, without bonds, or payments, but with only good strategy for knowing how to deceive those who trust them, they take out contracts for which in other parts much wealth would be required to start them and even more for the bid which they place.)

The reader returns to a similar situation in the episode with his second wife, Gracia, when Guzmán lives on her prostitution. The vicious and corrupt marriage is well matched by Guzmán's treatment of himself as a "prince":

Yo me trataba como un príncipe. Rodaban por la casa las piezas de plata, en los cofres no cabían las bordaduras y vestidos de varias telas de oro y seda, los escritorios abundaban de joyas preciosísimas. Nunca me faltó qué jugar, siempre me sobró con qué triunfar. Y con eso gozaban de su libertad. (Alemán 840)

(I treated myself like a prince. The pieces of silver rolled around the house, the clothes and embroideries of various fabrics of gold and silk did not fit into the coffers, the desks abounded in terrifically precious jewels. I never lacked [money] to gamble with, I always had enough in order to win. And they enjoyed their freedom [the people paying for Gracia].)

The person occupies a domestic space that receives the influences of the way he does business in the bourgeois society. Thus, Guzmán goes a step further than Lazarillo in terms of the economic definition of the self. The private person in *Lazarillo de Tormes* has an economic meaning in so far Lázaro considers his person to be the unification of a life whose purpose is to escape poverty. For Guzmán, his person in engaged in the expectation of richness and, therefore, in acquiring wealth. In both cases the person describes the centrality of social expectations in the mapping of an individual mind. These are social expectations that point to a state of potential mobility and to a re-structuring of the way this individual conceives his life and the life of his society.

As I argued in the previous chapter, the idea of self-determination as an attribute of a secularized person born with Lazarillo and given an explicit economic dimension with Guzmán begins to be attacked and finally defeated within the literature of the *pícaros*. The drive for unrestricted economic improvement becomes a fiction within a fiction, a dangerous illusion and social disease. The characters of these illusions, however, populate the literature of the *república* and, therefore, are impregnated with the traits and gestures of self-assertive persons; but they are not persons, they are essentially intruders and assailants of the rentier's order.

In my view López de Úbeda's Justina and Quevedo's Pablos mark the transition to this state of the matter. Whereas Justina's writing represents a critical distance from the authorial frame, Pablos's recounting of his own life is merely a superficial gesture devoid of any self-reflective attitude. The inscribed author lets Justina's provocative language display a satirical view of aristocratic conventions and even recuperate the bold and straight equation of sex and money from the tradition of *La Celestina*. Pablos's narration, however, is a demonstration of futile attempts at changing social identity. In Rico's words:

> El destino de la picaresca era malentender la lección del anónimo quinientista y de Mateo Alemán, volver al prejuicio de clase y a todo el cortejo de sus implicaciones en la jerarquía de las letras. *La vida del Buscón*, por próxima a los modelos y por eximia en otros aspectos, lo testimonia a las mil maravillas: ahí, presentar a Pablos como objeto de abyección y ridículo uniformes, limitarlo a una sola faceta peyorativa, es justamente presentarlo como miembro de una clase social, tipificarlo. (Rico 150-151)

> (The fate of the picaresque was to misunderstand the lesson by the anonymous from the fifteen-hundred and by Mateo Alemán, to return to class prejudice and all the implications for the hierarchy of the humanities. *La vida del Buscón*, close to its models and brilliant in some other aspects, is well example of it: there, to present Pablos as a uniform object of abjection and mockery, to limit him within a single pejorative feature is precisely to present him as a member of a social class, to typify him.)

This return to class prejudice makes it impossible for Pablos to become a person of his own. On the contrary, he remains from the beginning to the end a self-immolated outsider and a pathetic example of the road to crime. In this sense, he is the perfect transition to the rest of the literature of *pícaros* where the dissociation between the character and the narrator becomes a necessary ideological outcome of the seigniorial reaction.

A re-evaluation of the person had to wait, in my view, to Baltasar Gracián's writing for the few. His works make significant changes in both the fictionalization of an early civil society and the tradition of books of courtly manners. His high sophistication of language assumes a reader that does not merely enjoy the difficulty of linguistic games and the unveiling of hidden references, in the manner of López de Úbeda or even Quevedo. In addition to these requirements, Gracián's reader must look for an intellectual challenge, for an invitation to inquiry in himself the depth of his qualities to succeed in a hostile world.

If Lázaro's self-affirmation has to do with his realization that he possesses a person and a private life, Baltasar Gracián's writing strives, almost a century later, to elevate a select group of people over a society that seems to be left at the mercy of previously unknown forces. Maravall has properly described the relationship between *libre concurrencia* (free competition) and an early idea of self-interest:

> La 'libre concurrencia', cuyo principio en el XVI, nadie sabe formular y que está muy lejos todavía de regir los negocios humanos, es ya, sin embargo, en alguna medida, el régimen sin obstáculos en la lucha para imponer su propio valer a que aspira el humanista en el plano de la cultura o el mercader en el del comercio o el gobernante en el juego político pluriestatal. [...] Las versiones de pesimismo antropológico de Gracián o de Hobbes responden ajustadamente a esta situación, aunque ya en una etapa de consecuencias ulteriores respecto a los primeros cambios renacentistas. (Maravall, *Estado moderno*... I, 417-418)

> (Free competition that, born in the 16th century, nobody knows how to formulate and that is still far from ruling human business, is nevertheless, to some extent, the regime without obstacles in the struggle to impose one's own value to which the humanist aspires in the level of culture, or the merchant in the level of commerce, or the ruler in the political game within multiple states [...] Versions of anthropological pessimism in Gracián or Hobbes rightly react to this situation, though in a period of different consequences in relation to the first changes in the Renaissance.)

Instead of a pessimistic outlook, we might want to see a complex and positive attitude toward the formation of a self-reflective attitude in terms of a social distinction. The drive for growth has converted enrichment to the precondition of a new individualized value of the person in terms of "success":

> Cuando se busca el triunfo o el éxito se está buscando un añadido óntico, un enriquecimiento o perfección del ser humano, que tiene a su vez una repercusión social [...] El éxito así obtenido no ha de medirse pragmáticamente, sino ontológicamente, pues aunque el triunfo venga a través de la sociedad, es la persona la que queda elevada en su ser. (Abellán 55)

> (When one seeks success or victory, one is looking for an ontic addition, an enrichment or perfection of the human being, with a social transcendence [...] This success must not be measured pragmatically, but ontologically, because even though victory comes through society, it is the person who is elevated in his being.)

The attainment of success might discriminate ontologically the growth of the person. Yet, it really accomplishes a differentiation among *gentes* (people) that replaces the medieval ontology that discriminated between humans and animals:

> así lo más del mundo no son sino corrales de hombres incultos, de naciones bárbaras y fieras, sin policía, sin cultura, sin artes y sin noticias, provincias habitadas de monstruos de la herejía, de gentes que no se pueden llamar personas, sino fieras. (*Criticón* III, 234)
>
> (then, most of the world is the backyard of uneducated men, barbaric and ferocious nations, without order, without culture, without arts and without news, provinces inhabited by heretical monsters, by people who cannot be called persons but beasts.)

The person is the term reserved for a very small segment of the people of the world (now that the medieval "world" is expanding by commerce and trade to reach almost the whole planet) because the rest of *gentes* do not qualify for the attribute of self-determination. According to Gracián, they do not have culture, art, or *noticias* (news). The person has lost the basically Christian requirement of the participation with the divine, to accentuate the social requirements of culture and public display.

Against *gentes*, Gracián elevates the person to a superior cultural standing, which identifies some individuals as having "culture," a particular sensibility, knowledge of art and literature. These individuals are a few in the world:

> la plaza mayor del universo, pero nada capaz, llena de gentes, pero sin persona, a dicho de un sabio que con la antorcha en la mano, al medio día iba buscando un hombre que lo fuese y no había podido hallar uno entero. (*Criticón* II, 121)
>
> (the central plaza of the universe, but capable of nothing, crowded with people but with not a single person, according to a wise man who with a torch in his hand at noon was looking for a real man, but he could not find one in full.)

The person is a process of acquiring civility. Gracián is obviously breaking away from a purely theological perspective over the primacy of Christian revelation in the constitution of the person. His person lives among Christian people who, nevertheless, are not fully persons.

The means to success are embedded in the constitution of personal attributes: "Todo está en su punto y el ser persona en el mayor," he begins his *Oráculo manual y arte de prudencia* (143) (Everything is [requires] a skill and to be a person is the highest task). Gracián observes that in attaining a degree of superiority and distinction the person participates in a sensibility of the few. This sensibility results in and is reinforced by cultural activities such as a "noble conversación" (refined (noble) conversation):

> Es el hablar efecto grande de la racionalidad, que quien no discurre no conversa [...] Comunícase el alma noblemente produciendo conceptuosas imágenes de sí en la mente del que oye [...] De aquí es que las personas no pueden estar sin algún idioma común, para la necesidad y para el gusto [...] De suerte que es la noble conversación hija del discurso, madre del saber, desahogo del alma, comercio de los corazones, vínculo de la amistad, pasto del contento y ocupación de personas. (*Criticón* I, 13)
>
> (Talking is a great effect of rationality, because those who do not think cannot converse [...] The noble soul communicates producing conceptual images of itself in the listener's mind [...] It follows that persons need some common idiom, for the moments of need and pleasure [...] Thus, noble conversation is a daughter of discourse, mother of knowledge, relief of the soul, commerce of hearts, link of friendship, food of happiness and occupation of persons.]

This "occupation" of persons is not the state-dependent profession of the humanist writers or the *hombres de letras*. It is rather the activity of members of a society who privately aspire to develop a particular taste and knowledge:

> Gracián elaborates a new concept of the public man based on criteria of individual superiority, while reconfiguring the space and necessary apparatus for his public representation. Gracián's courtly philosophy is commensurate with the interests of public individuals belonging to the new elites at several levels: [...] by equating knowledge, moral superiority and humanity with power. [...] Gracián uses the word subjects to refer to a particular kind of animal entity, while reserving the term *persona* for a social construct whose meaning, whose being, comes about within the sphere of art... (Castillo 203)

In the search of success, this sphere of art does not differentiate between artistic production, in the narrow sense, and the production of skillful mechanisms of social interaction and aggression. The art of refined conversation and the art of becoming a person would seem to imply that Gracián considers the person to be a "mask" alluding to the ancient meaning of the term. On the contrary, his person is equivalent to the attainment of success, to the intentional elaboration of cultural attributes that can purposely be used in a social arena conceived in terms of subjugation and sovereignty.

Thus, the person acquires a political relevancy which was completely absent in Lázaro's life. We might say that Gracián's person observes a political horizon in the projection of his selective attributes of literary mastery and worldly heroism; this is a projection that formalizes his final enrichment: "tanto es uno cuanto sabe, y el sabio todo lo puede. Hombre sin noticias, mundo a oscuras." (*Oráculo manual*, 143) (one is what he knows, and the wise man is capable of everything. Man without news, world in darkness).

The hero and the discrete individual –Gracián's two figures of social success– still have the courtier's flavor of good manners and social propriety. They also respond to some extent to the intrigues in the palace to acquire privileges or favors in the bureaucracy of the seventeenth century. However, they are as well projections of the person in the formation of a political morality.

As projections of the person, the hero and the discrete individual rise above the *gentes* and the *vulgo*. In these figures the person gets close to the arena of political games by displaying the vocabulary of the struggle to command and avoiding defeat. The verbal and social skills of the person become the instruments of micro-battles within a world of permanent war:

> Pelea la sagacidad con estratagemas de intención: nunca obra lo que indica; apunta sí para deslumbrar; amaga al aire con destreza, y ejecuta en la impensada realidad, atenta siempre a desmentir. Echa una intención para asegurarse de la émula atención, y revuelve luego contra ella, venciendo por lo inesperado; pero la penetrante inteligencia la previene con atenciones; la acecha con reflejas: entiende siempre lo contrario de lo que quiere que entienda, y conoce luego cualquier intentar de falso: deja pasar toda primera intención y está en espera a la segunda, y aun a la tercera. (*Oráculo*, 146-147)

(Sagacity fights with strategies of intention: it never does what it indicates; indeed it aims in order to blind; it feigns skillfully in the air and then acts in an unexpected reality, always ready to contradict it. It throws an intention to make sure of a rival attention, and then comes back against it, wining by surprise; however, the sharp intelligence advises it with warnings; it watches with reflections: it always understands the opposite of what it is led to understand, and then perceives any false intention: letting the first intention pass, waiting for the second and even for the third.)

This is clearly a difficult conceptualization of what for Gracián seems to configure the nature of social life. The game of "intentions" seems to respond to the interest of the person in the defeat of his competitors. The state of war among individuals points to the realization in the self of the conditions that in the political order are determining the constitution of the State as the conflation between personal authority and the rational execution of force.

It is with the "person" that Hobbes exemplifies his concept of Sovereignty. He first defines the person along the lines of Christian theology: "A [Natural] Person, is he, whose words or actions are considered as his own." (Hobbes 111) He emphasizes, however, the self-determination of the person in his performance, verbally or socially, that results from being proprietor of his actions.

Above this natural person, Hobbes constructs the term of an "artificial person" as the political condition of the Sovereign: "And he that carries this Person, is called Sovereign, and said to have *Sovereign Power*; and every one besides, his Subject" (Hobbes 121).

We must note the sense of "possessing" and "holding" that the "artificial" person has in the sentence. Maravall has extensively argued that the conception of politics and political actions in terms of art or artificiality is one of the major distinctions of the implicit or explicit theorization of the formation of the State. The idea of a secular political order is further reinforced by the sense of creativity and technical construction, in the same vein that the functioning of the Monarchy is conceived as a "machine." As a technical creation, the personalization of authority implies not merely a personal possession of power, but rather that this higher "person" forcefully demands to act on and over all other subjects. Even though the concrete political circumstances of Spain and England differed greatly,

Maravall also indicated that an intellectual climate was ready in Spain for a similar conception of power:

> En España, no conozco en el siglo XVII ninguna influencia de Hobbes que pueda precisarse y definirse como tal. Sin embargo, esa tendencia a la totalización del poder político, que en otras partes fuera de Inglaterra, como hemos dicho, halló en la lectura de Hobbes un apoyo, en España se produjo de todas formas, favorecida seguramente por la ya acostumbrada utilización de un instrumento de dominio sobre las conciencias. (*Estado moderno...* I, 309)

(I do not know of any influence of Hobbes in Spain in the 17th century that we can clearly define as such. However, this tendency to a totalization of political power –which outside England found, as I said, a support in the reading of Hobbes– occurred anyway, probably because of the customary use of an instrument for the domination of people's mind.)

Gracián's person responds to this construction of sovereign power. His hero is the one who has attained the political virtue to be untouched and above the deadly struggles among many confrontational interests. His heroism is the result of a social process in which the person emerges within a field of strategically rational decisions or, as Gambin has put it, a "field of forces":

> "un campo de fuerzas, constituido por una pluralidad de relaciones consigo mismo y con el *otro* [que] afirma continuamente su propia contrariedad, su carácter provisional, transitorio, temporal." (Gambin 373)

(a field of forces constituted by a plurality of relationships with himself and the other, constantly affirming its own contradiction, its provisional, transitional and temporal characteristic.)

The person of the hero is the bearer of sovereignty, though his sphere of action is not the political order of the State, but the social space of individual self-affirmation. Gracián writes in his prologue to *El héroe* that the reader will find in his book "not a political or an economic, but rather a reason of state for yourself" ("una no política ni aun económica, sino una razón de estado de ti mismo").

(*El héroe* 5) The aim of the person is to conduct himself in a way that resembles the reflections and self-examinations that the State must do in order to maintain and reinforce its power. The "reason of state" of the person expresses the analogies between the government of the Monarchy and the government of individuals engaged in their own conditions of enrichment and conservation.

This reason provides the person with some of the virtues that directly protect his sovereignty. The understanding of motivations is the crucial art to unveil the hidden game of self-interest that permeates the world of exchanges, individual interactions and expectations. Knowledge of how to conduct one's own business implies also the knowledge of how to acquire information about others, their situation and the particular circumstances of social encounters.

The reason of the state of the person is a pervasive intellectual instrument for the attainment of the superior position he aspires to. It is this reason that helps the person to "live," in the sense that his life is the becoming of a social, artificial objective. As the state of the monarchy aspires to grant itself a reason to think and act above all other considerations for its own benefit, the reason of the person should as well be the finest accomplishment of self-preservation and success:

> No hay cosa que requiera más tiento que la verdad, que es un sangrarse del corazón [. . .] No todas las verdades se pueden decir: unas porque me importan a mí, otras porque al otro. (*Oráculo*, 198)
>
> (Nothing requires more care than truth, that is a bleeding of the heart [. . .] Not all truth can be told: some because they are important to me, others because they are important to the other.)

This strategic positioning of the person in a society conceived as a combat rationalizes in an elite language the social experiences of Lazarillo's and Guzmán's narration. Social life may be described as a field where the self-regulation of the actors is both the means to acquire things from others, as well as the awareness of the relevance of all aspects of the person in the pursuit of success.[4]

---

[4] Cf.: "It is by means of the cautious, essentially entrapment by immorality that the individual will become a *persona*." (Kassier 141)

The intellectual outlook of Gracián permits one to reach complex conclusions about a social world that Lázaro and Guzmán appreciated at the level of an economic reality. As Gracián's person elevates his social skills from the *gentes* and his tasteful understanding of art and literature above the *vulgo*, the world becomes a distant struggle empty of meaning and devoid of spiritual significance: "verás, finalmente, cuán mucha es la nada y que la nada querría serlo todo." (*Criticón* III, 222) (Finally, you will see how large is nothingness and how nothingness would like to be everything).[5]

The nothingness is the one engraved in the soul of the people, in the *vulgar* and blind movement toward to a false fulfillment. We are dealing again with the bourgeois complaint about the lack of individual virtue, and the need to transcend the illusory gratification of sensuality in order to attain a moral conduct able to aspire to harmonize with the purest and original Christian foundations. The view of "nothing" within the people, in society and across the world is the privilege of a person who emerges through an appropriation of the intellectual values that legitimize the monarchical state.

The development of the concept of the person along this period in Spain is marked by the historical circumstances that frame the emergence and establishment of an Absolute State. The conflictive trend expresses, however, the rupture with the Church as the only producer of a definition for the self-affirmation of individuals. The full force of the economic constitution of social exchanges emerges with Lázaro's anti-ecclesiastical satire and will continue with a growing conceptualization of the dialectical relations between a mercantile society and the private and domestic conducts.

Furthermore, the intellectualization of the person reflects a cultural level reached by bourgeois thought at the time that the State, in spite of the economic contradictions between rentier classes and merchant capital, assumes the conceptual mechanisms for the defense and growth of a self-interested conduct. A language of social

---

[5] Cf. also: "Mala señal, decía un discreto, cuando mis cosas agradan a todos; que lo muy bueno es de pocos, y el que agrada al vulgo, por consiguiente, ha de desagradar a los pocos, que son los entendidos." (*Criticón* II, 137) (It is a bad signal, says a discrete man, if my things please to everyone; a very good thing is for a few and, thus, the one who pleases the populace should displease the few who understand).

success intends to point to a self-differentiated area of knowledge in which "political" relations –artificial relations– are the expression of a superior understanding of moral and social dilemmas. Though Gracián would seem to think that these political relations are the result of a degradation from the ideals of heroic times, his advice to the hero and to the discrete man requires someone wiser than any previous man to heed them accordingly:

> Más se requiere hoy para un sabio que antiguamente para siete, y más es menester para tratar con un solo hombre en estos tiempos, que para todo un pueblo en los pasados. (*Oráculo manual* 143)
>
> (To be wise today requires more than was required for seven wise men in ancient times, and more is needed nowadays to deal with only one man than with a whole country in the past.)

The social perspective centered in this new personal heroism receives its full justification by the proposition that the requirements for political or intellectual success have reached a level unknown to the people of the past. The person must emulate the greatest accomplishments, which now stand as examples of means to conduct oneself among fierce competition and rivalry. The language of success, then, reveals a differentiated area of knowledge, one that is informed with a self-proclaimed intellectual heritage. This heritage serves the purpose of individualized micro-battles in the world.

The person excels in the hero in a way that Lazarillo could have not predicted. It creates, however, a distinction among people that was absent in the anonymous intention of 1554, when the affirmation of Lázaro's own person was directed at comparing favorably his life against the life of a nobleman. Gracián does not care much about this issue because he actually deals with an effective differentiation of people according to acquired values. Nonetheless, he presents his person within an order re-constructed by seigniorial hierarchies and under the deepening of Absolutism.

Chapter 3

A LITERARY SOCIETY WITHIN THE SEIGNIORIAL SOCIETY. CULTURE AND LIFE IN GRACIÁN

Ciudadano. El que vive en la ciudad y come de su hazienda, renta o heredad. Es un estado medio entre cavalleros o hidalgos, y entre los oficiales mecánicos. Cuéntase entre los ciudadanos los letrados, y los que professan letras y artes liberales. (Covarrubias 427-8)

(Citizen. The one who lives in the city and eats from his own possessions, rent or heritage. It is a middle state between noblemen or hidalgos and manual workers. We can count among the citizens the lawyers and those professionals of books and liberal arts.)

así lo más del mundo no son sino corrales de hombres incultos, de naciones bárbaras y fieras, sin policía, sin cultura, sin artes y sin noticias, provincias habitadas de monstruos de la herejía, de gentes que no se pueden llamar personas, sino fieras. (Gracián, *Criticón* III, 234)

(then, most of the world is the backyard of uneducated men, barbaric and ferocious nations, without order, without culture, without arts and without news, provinces inhabited by heretical monsters, by people who cannot be called persons but beasts.)

WITH the term *cultura* Gracián offers the notion of a social good that differs from civil regulations and order (*policía*) and from the arts. It is revealing that he does not mention in this context the order properly of the State (*gobierno*) as one of the distinguishing features of nations. Instead he points to the supposed lack of regulations and duties of civil life in the "barbaric" world.

This distinction probably has to do with the well-established idea that according to natural law all people, since they live in a community, have developed one or another form of government. It is not in the sphere of *dominium* where civilization shows a higher degree of development, but rather in the sphere of social life.

However, his distinction of *cultura* from both *policía* and the arts seems more relevant. This notion of culture, particularly its attribution to both men and nations, departs from its restricted use in relation to the agrarian cycles to become a symptom of a civic life. As opposed to the barbaric life of the *hombres incultos*, the civic life develops in a climate of learned persons that has in the book and the circle of writing and reading its material and symbolic legitimization.

The urban privileged classes conceived the humanist re-assessment of the values of classical Antiquity as a legacy of knowledge and authority to substitute the agrarian-feudal worldview of the knight. In England with the term 'culture' "from early sixteenth century on the tending of natural growth was extended to a process of human development" (Williams 87).[1] This metaphorical extension reflects the transition from an agrarian-based economy to an urban-centered one that accumulates the riches of the country land and progressively acquires the leading role in the articulation of the monarchical State.

By the culture of men and nations, Gracián seems to typify a literary civility that together with art, news and order transforms people –*gentes*– into persons. While *gentes* is the universal term for any people under a government, persons are the outcome of a dialectical process between the authors and receptors of civility.

The growing importance of large-scale trade and a financial economy coincides with the humanist interest in constructing a symbolic dimension of life in the city. The political values of Antiquity become the symbolic universe by which the social order of the city acquires a conceptualization of its own. The city is not just a physical place to inhabit but also and more importantly, it is a distinction that a community acquires by reaching a higher level of sat-

---

[1] "Culture –says Williams– as an independent noun, an abstract process or the product of such a process, is not important before late eighteenth century and is not common before the middle of nineteenth century. But the early stages of this development were not sudden." (Williams 88). He quotes Milton in 1660 who talks of the "government and culture."

isfaction. In one of the first treatises on the organization of the *república*, and before political economists appear on the scene to address the bourgeois society, Alonso de Castrillo clearly states in 1521 that the city offers a better satisfaction of economic needs and higher level of civility:

> Entre todas las congregaciones de las gentes que tienen ocupado el mundo, sola la compañía de la cibdad sentimos ser la más noble y de más alto merecimiento. [. . .]; porque en la cibdad se halla la conversación más dulce y más noble, y las cosas necesarias a la vida se hallan más convenientes y con menos trabajo. (Castrillo 19-24)

> (Among all the congregations of peoples that inhabit the world, we feel that only the company of the city is the most noble and the one with a highest distinction [. . .]; because in the city there is the sweetest and most noble conversation, and the necessary things for life are found with convenience and less work.)

Cities enjoy a refined conversation and a higher standard of living in relation to other types of "congregations" of people. Commerce and trade alleviates the effort to satisfy their economic needs. Moreover, justice in life and a domesticated conversation are conditions a town must meet in order to acquire the dignity of a city: "De manera que si entre los cibdadanos es la vida justa y la conversación mansa, será el pueblo digno de ser llamado cibdad." (Castrillo 28) (Thus, if there is a just life and a refined conversation among the citizens, the town will warrant being called a city). Thus, a greater distribution of the economic life among citizens parallels, from its inception, the civic life of an educated "conversation" among these same people interested in a particular way of life that differs from the order of the political *dominium*:

> La República es una cierta orden o manera de vivir instituída y escogida entre sí por los que viven en la misma cibdad. (Castrillo 28-9)

> (The Republic is a particular order or way of life instituted and chosen by those who live in the same city.)

The urban-centered economic exchange makes possible a greater accumulation of things needed for life that frees the cities from the scarcities that typically define the conditions of a feudal system. For the privileged groups, an economy of "abundance" realized through commerce begins to supplant the self-sufficient economy of the estate system:

> This commercial exchange developed according to rules which certainly were manipulated by political power; yet a far reaching network of horizontal economic dependencies emerged that in principle could no longer be accommodated by the vertical relationships of dependence characterizing the organization of domination in an estate system based upon a self-contained household economy. (Habermas 15)

This "far reaching network of horizontal economic dependencies" will set the stage for the emergence of a bourgeois society. The urban-centered conception of a bourgeois society is by necessity the first step in the formulation of an economic space that by the end of the sixteenth century has already acquired a national intention. When in 1600 González de Cellorigo publishes his *Memorial*, by the "república de España" he means the social and moral implications of the state of the economy.

As I argued in a previous chapter, Luis Ortiz writes in 1558 on the relationship between monetary flow and commercial growth in response to the concerns for the welfare of the *repúblicas*. He has in mind the functioning of the economic order of the cities in so far as these cities have developed a differentiated society. This is the differentiated society that for González de Cellorigo, and many others after him, becomes the subject of a political economy.

The *república* is the particular way of life of the economic welfare of certain people who are able to develop among them a civic relationship. The refined conversation that Castrillo sees in the city-*república*, a century later in Gracián has a more qualified status. Gracián grants the "conversation" with the power to produce a higher participatory space for the persons:

> Es el hablar efecto grande de la racionalidad, que quien no discurre no conversa [...] Comunícase el alma noblemente produciendo conceptuosas imágenes de sí en la mente del que oye [...] De aquí es que las personas no pueden estar sin algún idioma común, para la necesidad y para el gusto [...] De suerte que es la noble conversación hija del discurso, madre del saber,

desahogo del alma, comercio de los corazones, vínculo de la amistad, pasto del contento y ocupación de personas. (*Criticón* I, 13)

(Talking is a great effect of rationality, because those who do not think cannot converse [. . .] The noble soul communicates producing conceptual images of itself in the listener's mind [. . .] It follows that persons need some common idiom, for the moments of need and pleasure [. . .] Thus, noble conversation is a daughter of discourse, mother of knowledge, relief of the soul, commerce of hearts, link of friendship, food of happiness and occupation of persons.]

Literary conversation seems to be, then, a feature of culture by which some people acquire the attributes of persons. This culture lies properly within the network of horizontal relations or, in other words, within the sphere of private exchanges in differentiation from the "public" domain of the State. In distinction to this public domain, the symbolic goods of culture constitute a civic exchange within the *república* of commercial dealings.

From the figure of the Renaissance's "courtier" to Gracián's worldly hero, the transition from social manners to culture parallels the increasing differentiation of a bourgeois literary society. The manners of the courtier cover a broad spectrum of verbal sophistication, social etiquette and poetic skills. His distinction serves as a role model for the high echelons of the monarchy, particularly since he portrays a conduct far removed from the needs of work and worldly affairs.

Gracián's hero shows some of these features but in a context where a literary society claims to bear a status of its own and a particularized function within the seigniorial society. This is the function of a "literary republic" where learned people acquire the identity of persons by the participation in an exchange of *letras*.

Although the doctrines of the Church and the values of an estate system still dominate this republic of symbolic goods, Gracián's depiction of a worldly hero identifies the cultural and political elements that explain the disintegration of the world of the courtier. Alban Forcione sees in this disintegration the representation of a loss of harmony and a "cosmic" indifference to a human quest for universal fulfillment. In this context, Gracián's person is:

> unaware that he is disintegrating constantly, helplessly prey to the arbitrary movements of the machinery of time and death, the

emblems of the ultimate meaning of a universe that has fallen silent. (Forcione, "At the Threshold of Modernity..." 47)

The confidence on the humanist tradition fades away while a perception of a formless world replaces the intellectual drive for plenitude and proportion. Maravall observed that Gracián's pessimism has, however, a political and anthropological dimension that responds to a feeling of instability and confrontation. The nascent individuation of economic and social demands transforms any organic vision of the person into a monadic universe where social expectations actually participate in the relative dissolution of the legitimization of a stratification based on lineage. These transformations result, according to A. Cascardi, in a process of personal relations that, however, are still subject to the exemplary model conduct of a "society of the court":

> Gracián's observations must be understood in the context of a world that is critical of, but nonetheless still dominated by, the society of the court. The model of social relations exemplified in courtly society carries forward the principles of absolute distinctions and 'exemplary' relations characteristic of a hierarchical society into an environment where they are tested by the increasingly verbal, psychological, and individualizing nature of personal relations. (Cascardi 255)

This "society of the court" is the circle of seigniorial and ecclesiastical groups that, together with the higher echelons of the royal administration, benefit from a system of privileges in exchange for crediting the monarchy with their public display of economic and symbolic power. This society reinforces the subordination of social conduct to monarchical authority while assuming the need for a more calculated strategy of the linguistic expression of the person's goals.

In the process, a secularized and rationalist perspective intends to overcome the tension between transcendent ideas and those political drives that, individually oriented, break through a feudal organism that identifies the self with a mythical foundation. Verbal sophistication and a calculated personal strategy permit a degree of self-reflection on the value of symbolic tools: the value of a social interaction conducted, to a very important degree, by and through products of the intellect.

A political person emerges within the seigniorial society at those particular moments when participation in its organic structure also requires the actual acquisition of privileges. Thus, competitive features of an emergent bourgeois society pervade these moments of the society of the court, specifically in the way its learned members invest in literary abilities and verbal emulation and rivalry.

Though subordinated to the seigniorial society, the literary republic begins to develop a sensibility closer to a bourgeois demand for the representation of private advancement and conservation. The imaginary reproduction of identities tends to move beyond essential definitions of social exchanges, toward a valorization of personal attributes where culture progressively replaces the values of lineage or origin.

Juan Carlos Rodríguez sees in the narration of the *pícaro*'s origin an ideological matrix where the new bourgeois ideology confronts the feudal legitimization of social and economic relations:

> Planteadas toda serie de interrogaciones en torno al famoso autobiografismo picaresco, lo importante es señalar cómo en el texto del *Lazarillo* se van desplegando –y reproduciendo– todos los valores, toda la lógica de la nueva ideología animista burguesa que es la que a la vez "produce" –como decimos– el texto mismo: no sólo su "yo" explícito sino toda la temática de lo "privado" en general, tal y como subyace determinando la estructura del texto. (Rodríguez 129)

> (With all kinds of questions regarding the famous picaresque autobiography, the important thing is to point out that the text of *Lazarillo* deploys and reproduces all the values, the whole logic of the new animist, bourgeois ideology, which in turn "produces" –as we are saying– the text itself: it is not only the explicit "I" but also the whole theme of the "private" in general, in the way it is immersed in and determines the textual structure.)

The literary life, according to Rodríguez, emerges when the *vida propia* –one's own life– begins to inform the needs of a bourgeois self. In other words, literature emerges, to a certain extent, as a means to conceptualize changes in a social legitimization based on the symbolic structure of an estate society.

A properly bourgeois mentality interacts within the patrimonial structure of the seigniorial society. In this context, the space of *le-*

tras becomes the symbolic product of and the material base to a social practice in which the display of sophisticated manners sets the stage for a "linguistic complexity" and a conceptual and verbal artifice:

> The court is a kind of stock exchange; as in every "good society," an estimate of the "value" of each individual is continuously being formed. But here his value has its real foundation not in the wealth or even the achievements or ability of the individual, but in the favor he enjoys with the king, the influence he has with other mighty ones, his importance in the play of courtly cliques. (Elias 271)

Elias's metaphor to describe the "society of the court" as a kind of stock exchange characterizes very well not only the structural dependence of that society to a commercial-financial complex dominated by merchant cities, but also the broader cultural significance of an exchange of "immaterial" goods.[2]

Culture, then, refers to a variety of civic processes closely related to an idea of a "personal reason" derived from the new political paradigm of the "reason of the State." At the peak of the process of the formation of the State as a self-sufficient mechanism that seeks to find in itself the reason for its existence, Baltasar Gracián writes his *Hero* to offer "not a political or an economic, but rather a reason of state for yourself" ("una no política ni aun económica, sino una razón de estado de ti mismo"). (*El héroe* 5) He intends to provide a normative model of conduct based on a description of a state of affairs in which every social exchange may result in damage for the person.

---

[2] Elias's study assumed the thesis that the modern state is the outcome of a process of "feudalization" initiated in the Late Middle Ages. However, at some point he recognizes how the dynamics of commerce and monetary dealings transformed a stratification according to patrimonial power into an interdependence according to money: "Under the pressure of competitive struggles of a particular stage and structure, the demand for money increases at this time; to satisfy it new ways and means are sought and found. But, as was pointed out earlier, this movement has a very different meaning for different sectors of society; precisely this shows how great the functional interdependence of different strata has become. Favored by this movement are all those groups whose functions permit them to compensate for the falling purchasing power of money by acquiring more money, i.e., above all bourgeois groups and the controllers of the tax monopoly, the kings." (Elias 265)

This situation can revert to the person's benefit if he calculates his actions as well as his words. For that purpose Gracián's manuals of conduct and his allegorical novel *El criticón* attempt to define the scope of a political morality that would provide the person with some rules for his social engagement.

In the realm of kingdoms, this reason of state emerges in conflict with the alliance between patrimonial domination and Medieval Christian doctrine. A reason of state emerges through an effort to rationalize the power of the Monarchy in terms of a performance of the different parts of a mechanical whole:

> En su virtud, el Estado y el mismo poder, cuanto más organizados, más objetivados se reconocen respecto al arbitrio del príncipe y del equipo de gobernantes. El Estado, cuanto más se somete a organización, más aparece como mecanismo que sigue su propio movimiento, según las combinaciones de sus resortes [. . .] Esta visión de la política estatal renacentista ha impuesto a quienes se han ocupado de ella la imagen del reloj: el mundo aparece concebido como una maquinaria, como un aparato de relojería que lleva su propio movimiento, si bien necesita con frecuencia la experta intervención del relojero para rectificarlo. La naturaleza, dijo Vives (*De prima philosophia*, I), es como una máquina automática, un reloj o cualquier otro aparato semejante. (Maravall, *Estado moderno y mentalidad social* I, 56-7)

> (By its own constitution, the more organized the State and power itself are the more objective they are considered to be in relation to the prince and the team of the government. The more the State is submitted to an organization, the more it looks like a mechanism that follows its own movement according to the combinations of its springs [. . .] This vision of the Renaissance's politics of the State has produced the image of a clock for those who have thought about it: the world seems to be conceived like a machine, a clock-like apparatus with its own movement, though it frequently needs the skilful intervention of the watchmaker to correct it. Nature, Vives said (*De prima philosophia*, I), is like an automatic machine, a clock or any other similar apparatus.)

In relation to the person too, political conduct requires a rationalization of social performance. Self-conservation and advancement are the contents of an individualized knowledge that Gracián describes as the "knowledge of how to live." As I argued previously, the cultural nature of this "life" must be measured in terms of success. This is in terms of the real possibilities for the attainment of a higher position for the person. This higher position encompasses both the accomplishment of concrete privileges and a better strategic situation from which to reach a superior social space.

The worldly hero is the exemplary person that bears a concept of achievement tuned to the expectations of bureaucratic élites and the ambitions of wealth-seekers. In this regard, Gracián's figure of the hero has an intellectual and a practical dimension: "¿De qué sirve el saber si no es práctico? Y el saber vivir es hoy el verdadero saber." (*Oráculo manual* 212-213) (What is the purpose of knowledge if it is not practical? To know how to live is today the true knowledge). This hero responds to the challenges of his life by developing a personal knowledge of the broader conditions of individual confrontations through verbal virtuosity and intellectual competition.

The literary discourse of life –the *vida* of picaresque narratives and the *vivir* of Gracián– begins to represent a political morality of the person that builds on both the verbal display of the seigniorial society and the bourgeois drive for private accomplishments.

THE POLITICAL LIFE OF THE PERSON

In this sense, the *pícaro* Guzmán de Alfarache in the novel by Mateo Alemán presents his life as the process by which to achieve a balance between deeds and errors; between the demands of a Feudal-Christian world and the needs imposed by a mercantile society. The discourse of his life resembles in many aspects the ethical and economic concerns addressed in the writings of jurists and *memorialistas* regarding the state of the *república*. Life as a concept of social growth involves both the development of a personal private life and the projection of this person within the circuit of economic exchanges.

With the life of a person in *Lazarillo de Tormes* and *Guzmán de Alfarache* social relations are the result of an intentionally and individually oriented acquisition or conservation of economic goods. The *pícaro* Guzmán allows us to see a calculation that involves actions and people in order to attain a better economic position. His economic definition sustains the process of his life even in those conflicts that express aristocratic or religious values. In the discourse of the *pícaro*'s life, these values are appearances through which the economic conflict unfolds *symbolically*.

In Gracián appearances constitute a symbolic field where the person individually defends his privileges within a patrimonial structure of power subjected to the imperial monarchy. These privileges cover an array of personal favors, pretensions of ennoblement, tax and financial benefits, influences in the decision-making institutions, as well as art and literary sponsoring.

The person, in Gracián, must be alert to the "segundas intenciones" –"double intentions"– coming from competitors and must develop a strategy of response to overcome the attack in a particular conjuncture. In this sense, literary creation is a reflective product of the verbal strategies and intentional misunderstandings that the person faces within the symbolic field of his social environment. To this effect, Gracián names with the term *refleja* –reflection– the working of a strategic ability of the mind that unveils the multiple intentions or meanings in a social conjuncture. It is the same ability that, when functioning with the poetic or rhetorical faculty of *agudeza* –sharpness–, is able to both produce and decode a literary discourse constructed by a multi-layered meaning.

A symbolic wealth circulates through this field of appearances and intentions whose ultimate meaning lies in the status of the person and his qualifications to increase his precarious standing. Certain sophistication in the *arts* of prudence and *agudeza* corresponds to the particular status the person has acquired in his social performance and, then, to the level of symbolic wealth he is able to stimulate or pretend to possess. The appearance of wealth is, in this context, one of the major impulses of his wealth since it is within the field of apparent meanings where the conjuncture is resolved.

A provisional or apparent victory is also the foundation of additional verbal and rhetorical resources for the next social encounter. The person must realize that there is never a definitive victory; on the contrary, there is always an unfriendly move waiting to strike at the slightest symptom of inattentiveness.

The capacity for observation and for detecting hidden movements and meanings is truly an art of self-government that aspires to emulate the self-given reason of state. The theoretical signification of this political practice was initiated by Machiavelli's elaboration of sovereignty in terms of the capacity to instrumentalize all values in order to maintain a prince's state:

> "You must realize this: that a prince, and especially a new prince, cannot observe all those things which give men a reputation for virtue, because in order to maintain his state he is often forced to act in defiance of good faith, of charity, of kindness, of religion [...] So let a prince set about the task of conquering, and maintaining his state; his methods will always be judged honorable and will be universally praised. The common people are always impressed by appearance and results." (Machiavelli 57-8)

The relationship between virtue and vice, which is said to constitute the identity of the moral person, acquires a different meaning when observed from the perspective of political conduct. Moreover, this political conduct is the consequence of a translation of the moral person to a conjuncture that requires above all a rationalization of his goals:

> And then, he (the Prince) must not flinch from being blamed for vices which are necessary for safeguarding the state. This is because, taking everything into account, he will find that some of the things that appear to be virtues, if he practices them, ruin him, and some of the things that appear to be vices will bring him security and prosperity. (Machiavelli 50)

The person assumes a different position –a different "place" Gracián says– in relation to both his moral structure and his relation to others. The translation of the moral person to a political conjuncture does not erase his participation in transcendent values but it does open a parallel field of validation for the means to deploy in search of his goals. The "reason of state" as well as Gracián's "reason of state for yourself" have their roots in this new position the person becomes aware of by and through his social performance.

The prince as well as Gracián's hero a century later differentiate moral actions according to their capacity to influence this new position of the person: "Prudence –says Machiavelli– consists in being able to assess the nature of a particular threat and in accepting the lesser evil." (Machiavelli 74). Gracián assumes Machiavelli's legacy on prudence in relation to the life of a hero who confronts other strategies and other intentions, all of them directed to acquire a civil sovereignty over him. If the person aspires to succeed he must conduct his life keeping a balance (a calculation) between an absolute notation of moral values and a relative structure of secular intentions.[3]

The affirmation of the sovereignty of the person is the goal of Gracián's recommendations for a successful new hero, the prudent and discrete man of affairs. The successful conduct requires an assessment of the particular situation the person confronts: "Sea ésta la primera destreza en el arte de entendidos, medir el lugar por su artificio." (*El héroe* 7) (This is the most important skill in the art of those with knowledge: one must measure the place according to its artifice).

The place –*lugar*– seems to refer to the concrete and particular conditions of a social exchange. The *artificio* –artifice– refers to the mechanical and intentionally calculated actions of the actors of the exchange. Actions oriented to extract a benefit do not follow essential or substantial conceptions of virtue or vice, Gracián implies, but rather they are subjected to the conjuncture of a particular confrontation.

The "artifice of the place" captures the image of a complex set of performances through which the person conducts his worldly affairs. As opposed to "natural" substantiality, the artifice is a construction of potentially deceitful meaning; in other words, the artifice does not disclose its meaning in a straightforward way but after a careful observation of its mechanical functioning. It can be argued that some major literary genres and styles such as collections of emblems and the complex working of the *conceptos* –conceits– ground their expectations in the belief that social conduct and intellectual goods are devoid of truth regarding the world of human beings.

Gracián's art of a political life recreates –at a more formal level– the secularization of conduct that Alemán's *pícaro* painfully sought

---

[3] Obviously, there seems to be a difference between Machiavelli's and Gracián's notion of prudence, which has to do with the place that Christian doctrine has in the latter. One can argue that while for Machiavelli political conduct is a desirable objective, for Gracián it is the consequence of a morally degraded world. However, this difference in their respective religious outlooks is less relevant for the characterization of the person than the acceptance of the need to rationalize his conduct according to his self-interest.

to articulate by means of a religious-economic account of his life, and that *Lazarillo de Tormes* initiated earlier with a discourse on his own person. The picaresque narratives focus, though, on poverty, social mobility and enrichment as the central issues of the self-affirmation of the person. Their economic life is the referent of the changing nature of all other values, thus becoming the cause of both moral deception and personal opportunities.

A new "place" for the new actors of the *república* expresses then their economic needs *and* the transformations in the legitimate means of symbolic and linguistic articulation of these needs. This is a place constructed on the basis of the greater geographical and social mobility made possible by the growing mercantile structure. In this sense, it is a place that tends to induce changes and eventually replace the seigniorial privileges of a system of estates.

Gracián indicates that there is a new place for the person also in terms of his cultural and linguistic "position" for advancement and competition. Regarding his worldly and secular intentions, the person performs in a differentiated setting from his exclusively religious origin. His eventual success occurs in the realm of both money and language, as they are acquisitions –goods– and devices for asserting his value among others.

As I showed previously regarding the transition from the institutional space of the Church to the secular case represented by *Lazarillo*, property is an essential distinction of the person. He owns his life in such radical and unique way that he dares to write about it and to openly propose its higher value above members of the nobility. His material goods, however, fall short of matching his aspirations of economic improvement. Property for Lázaro remains at the level of a gesture of authenticity and, ironically, as a dubious accommodation.

In *Guzmán*, on the contrary, property is a long-life goal and a partial accomplishment. I tried to show that his person is the responsible party at play in Guzmán's economic transactions. Person and property, for him, are intimately united because Guzmán already operates within a mercantile mentality, which, as I shall argue next chapter, accepts the ambivalence and simultaneity of religious and material wealth in the very same field of a secular life.

For Machiavelli too the struggle around property disengages the economic conduct from all other kinds of loyalties: "But above all a prince must abstain from the property of others; because men sooner forget the death of their father than the loss of their property." (Machiavelli 54)

It is easy to detect a feeling of regret in this statement that may serve by itself to dispel the idea of an amoral Machiavelli. He nevertheless points to the *reality* of his observation, the fact that property ranks first in the spirit of men.[4] In this sense, his manual of conduct for the prince is a theory of how to accomplish his goals in a world where people do not hold on to the teleological values of an agrarian community or kinship.

The *pícaro* Guzmán writes the discourse of his life in order to tell something similar. His story attempts to articulate the description of economic drives together with a traumatic perception of the relative status of religious values. As I show in chapter four, this articulation takes the question of wealth and enrichment to a symbolic or intellectual level. The *pícaro*'s virtues and vices acquire a definite meaning in relation to personal growth, in spite of the fact that he strives to maintain their ultimate participation in a transcendent order.

In his perspective, his life is the discursive effort to distinguish his experiences while in search for social mobility from a seigniorial and ecclesiastical system of privileges. Guzmán's attempts at economic independence seldom escape the bondage of the master-servant relationship, and when it does escape his ambitions of economic welfare are frustrated by a financial-legal framework that tends to benefit lords and masters. The burden of a feudal relation impairs his blows to the seigniorial authority and its stratified process of social mobility.

In order to share his perspective one must view his life from the process of his writing and from the position of Guzmán, the writer. Within a different line of argumentation Peter Dunn has stated clearly: "So it is in his self-awareness as writer of his life that Guzmán achieves the unity of recollection, thought, and act." (Dunn 196).

From this point of his life, the *pícaro*'s account merges with Gracián's later description of the worldly hero. Gracián's *picaresca*

---

[4] Machiavelli observes that political conduct arises from the need to face and encounter "real" forces. "Therewith, in next to no time, the meaning of all the elements of the conjuncture changes: they become real or potential forces in the struggle for the historical objective, and their relations become *relations of force*." (Althusser 19)

pura –"pure picaresque' in the characterization of Montesinos– attempts to abstract the successful conduct of the new hero out of the deceitful world of intentional wrongdoing and untruthful appearances. Gracián's hero has the worldly knowledge that the *pícaro* acquires only at the peak of his degradation –when a prisoner in the galleys– and while writing his perspective. Alemán's life of a *pícaro* participates of the same writing through which the old aristocratic courtier will become, in Gracián, the hero that strives to acquire and maintain the unstable privileges of the seigniorial society.

Gracián offers the wisdom and the art of a sophisticated conduct that the *pícaro*'s *writing*, by opening the perspective from which to examine his life, aspires to achieve. The art to compete for benefits, favors and patronage that implicitly pervades the hero's verbal display and strategic performance, is the intellectual counterpart of the lessons that the *pícaro*'s *life* teaches once this life is viewed from his writing.

The *pícaro*'s writing, in distinction to his life, displays a knowledge that, while it was absent in his life, now makes possible the representation of that life as a process of striving to acquire that knowledge. His life comes forward in his writing as an intellectual process to reconcile seigniorial and ecclesiastical values with commercial virtues. This intellectual process becomes explicit in the written articulation of the different stages of a life that seemed to run blind and senseless. The *pícaro*'s writing intends to explain the moral and economic tendencies that in a contradictory way shaped his conduct and his goals. In other words, it is in the function of a writer that the *pícaro* Guzmán may obtain the knowledge that the rest of the people lack.

His culture is his literary ability to provide a picture of social engagements through a rationalized account of an interaction of people based on mutually deceptive intentions. Gracián's hero assumes this state of affairs in order to acquire a superior condition of distinction and self-control.[5] His self-control is the product of the knowledge of himself attained by the observation of and judgments on other people.

---

[5] Cascardi has even argued that this model of self-control is directly related to the self-inflected repression that is at the roots of a bourgeois subject: "The 'prudent man's' ideals are characterized by his self-imposed moderation and restraint as well as by the control of desire required in the rationalized bourgeois world." (Cascardi 258).

The hero aims at a personal sovereignty that actualizes in the sphere of culture the power of rationalization of the state. The competition for acquiring and maintaining privileges, and accessing superior instances of power requires his conduct to be informed by an accurate knowledge of the circumstances and people involved in a particular social exchange.

Knowledge, for the hero, is concretely the knowledge that leads to reason according to his own personal investment in cultural goals and according to a state of affairs constituted by different personal positions. A rationalization of both, his investment and the state of affairs must conclude with a charting of the possibilities for action, victory and defeat; in other words, a charting of a world of intellectual competition.

Competition of the intellectual faculties becomes the way of life for the person, his own "reason of state." In this context, for Gracián the literary society gives a cultural form to the social practices that are based on verbal skills and rhetoric. The literary society represents these practices and contributes originally to arm the person with the conceptual tools needed to observe and assess the nature of intellectual competition.

Thus, Gracián's idea of culture is embedded in and derives from writing as the grounding of its artifice and the concrete product of the intellectual level of social exchanges, the level that properly belongs to persons. This culture of writing is the accomplishment of humanists and men of letters, the product that validates their search for their own social space and position along the boundaries between the political and the bourgeois societies.

Writing itself was the skill with which to aspire to social mobility and reputation. Writing was a particular form of wealth that the humanist man of letters could invest in to acquire prestige (Fame) and to participate in the symbolic validation of the political reason of state. [6] They naturally find themselves in an intellectual alliance

---

[6] The break with the ecclesiastical limits of writing is a long process that, having been initiated in the Late Middle Ages, properly defines the role of the man of "letters" as a differentiated activity from the Scholastic philosopher or the theologian: "las letras que estudian estos humanistas no son ya el descanso del guerrero. Los humanistas aspiran a intervenir directamente en el gobierno, buscan el poder." (Yndurain 76) [the writing that these humanists study are not the relief of the knight any more. Humanists aspire to intervene directly in the government, they want the power.]

with a mercantile sensibility, as Martin saw studying the conditions of the Italian Renaissance:

> Thus, in many ways there was a close correlation between the mercantile classes and the intelligentsia. They shared a common bourgeois origin and had complementary interests: in the former instance social prestige, in the latter material and social support; they had a common attitude and were brought together by the inherent objective and stylistic relationship of money and intellect. (Martin 41)

The relation of money and intellect covers more than a strictly economic sphere. It also and foremost distinguishes the function of a literary society as a particular form of wealth, a particular form of social differentiation and accumulation of symbolic goods. The intellect circulates among the literary society as a good in itself and as a means to satisfy the need for a self-definition of persons.

This conceptualization of the intellect as an instrument of struggle permeates political discourse and the literary society. Writing itself becomes a *tour de force*, a demonstration of wit and rhetorical cleverness. The artifice of writing, Gracián suggests, parallels the political conduct of the person as this conduct parallels the artifice of the machine of the state. The artifice in all cases is the outcome of molding a difficult meaning into a complex set of references. This intellectual emphasis in personal relations is a definite feature of the conceptualization of culture developed by the urban and courtly élites in their effort to sustain their particular function within the monarchy:

> the writer of fiction who [. . .] was among the earliest of the cultural workers to see the product of his/her labor achieve a certain degree of autonomy from the previously implicit mode of production, communication, and circulation of his/her activity was faced with two immediate problems: the autonomization of this production had to be recognized and then legitimized. The emergence of the notion of 'literature' as a designator for the autonomous area of the sphere of culture was a response to the first problem. (Godzich and Spadaccini 43)

Literature, in other words, acquires for the first time a cultural status on its own right. Certain élites develop a sense of differentiation from marginal or excluded groups that permit a self-reflection on their personal distinction from their social milieu. [7] A literary culture –essentially the writing of a political and economic morality of the person– provides a distinctive intellectual practice for the individuals who see themselves as members of a *república*, an exchange of art and artifice, and a competition of virtuous –that is profitable– conducts.

The literary society, as a particular and increasingly autonomized sphere of the seigniorial society, is informed by the fact that its linguistic and rhetorical dimensions are also means for a social distribution of wealth and privileges. Analyzing the role of language and education during the Humanist period, Malcolm Read argues that:

> Social divisions are most effective when marked and reinforced by language. In the sixteenth century, relevant barriers divided the literate from the illiterate, Latinists from non-Latinists, and those who controlled relevant dialects, registers and styles from those that did not. Such linguistic differences were exploited by different classes and class fractions to establish and preserve basic social divisions. (Read, "Language, Education and the Absolutist State" 14)

The tendency toward a self-justification of literature as a socially relevant cultural product within the larger space of exchange of the *república* motivates the production of an immense number of books directed to a cultivated person. This literary event occurs through conditions of an expanded exchange process. The expansion of trade furnishes the communicative framework to actualize supra-local perceptions of human interaction, cosmopolitan feelings of art and writing, and political and philosophical ideas for the educated people.

For these educated people the society that they begin to conceive in competitive terms is still a "world," an entity made of seigniorial

---

[7] "By means of this process of confluence and differentiation at a higher level, 'literature' becomes a cultural product in its own right. As such, it enables, first, the formation of a cultural field in which 'cultivated' individuals begin to develop a sense of 'taste' or 'distinction' on the basis of the distribution, reading, and discussion of literary works. Second, it permits individual acts of self-reflection on one's own position in a social arena increasingly perceived as opposed, and sometimes in contradiction, to one's private and intimate realms." (Lewis and Sánchez XI-XII)

institutions and religious determinations. The literary world, as well as the world of the government and the spiritual world are composites of individual drives for recognition and success, and of a mechanical organicism in which, for good or evil, everything is related to the whole.

The economic nature of the *república* spreads over these worlds coloring their symbolic goods with the worldly life of private exchanges in search of profit. In Gracián's description these exchanges are the testing realm of a microcosm of a civic sovereignty: "Si todo exceso en secreto lo es en caudal, sacramentar una voluntad será soberanía." (*El héroe* 8) (Since excess in secret is also an excess in wealth, sealing [blessing] the will is sovereignty)

In chapter four I analyze the function of the term *caudal* in Alemán's *Guzmán* and in Gracián's texts within a representation of both the material and the symbolic dimensions of wealth. In Gracián the term informs of a mercantile sensibility that perceives intellectual processes as an important source of wealth to invest in verbal skills, reputation and in a prudent conduct. This symbolic wealth makes possible the development of a personal sovereignty that, for Gracián, is the highest accomplishment of the intellectual world. By the interrelation of the competitive nature of the intellectual world together a culture of persons and the development of a literary society, a new concept of social relations seems to emerge where individuals are valued in terms of their merit and distinction.

The "world" that still permeates notions of social relations is the result of the theological division between the profane and the sacred. In this context, the "world" is either the expression of the eternal working of the divine or, in the more authoritarian ecclesiastical notion, is the temporal and finite state of the Christian person. Thus, Covarrubias in 1611 defines the world as the "temporal" relations between laymen:

> Mundo: El trato de aquellos que atienden tan sólo a las cosas temporales, y a éstos llamamos mundanos. Algunas vezes mundo sinifica [sic] la instabilidad de las cosas, y la mudança dellas, y de los estados. (Covarrubias 819)

> ([the world] is the dealings of those [people] who only look after temporal things, and we call them worldly people. Sometimes, world means the instability of things and how they and the estates change.)

From the point of view of the Christian doctrine, temporal relations are relations whose object does not have a sacred quality. Covarrubias also points to the ever-changing nature of these temporal things and the estates, an idea that rules the political imaginary of Christendom from the late Middle Ages on. The temporal (finite) nature of worldly dealings implies that, in spite of its distance from the divine, the world is mysteriously subject to the Providence, the eternal world.

In a significant departure from this position, the notion of artifice offers a distinctive and secular knowledge of "life" to the intellectual world and the literary *república*. Artifice is both in the object and the subject of the social exchange. It is in the object in the sense that verbal, social and literary exchanges are produced under an intentional complexity of meaning. Artifice is also a feature of the subject in the sense that people's intentions are always beyond the reach of clarification.

Intentions in human exchanges reinforce the underlining process by which social nature looses its substance, becoming a semi-artificial sphere and acquiring, therefore, the potential for a self-centered endless transformation and increasing plasticity. Joan Ramon Resina, in relation to Cervantes's re-structuring of a failing 'totality,' has properly seen:

> In an undecidable world where intentionality is the only stable truth, subjectivity becomes the space where a value-ground can be rediscovered and world-formation renewed. ("Cervantes's Confidence Games..." 244)

For Gracián, writing is the exemplary product of this artificial and intentional nature of verbal relations. As a product of relations between persons, the *república* of letters of the seventeenth century configures something close to what Habermas has called the "bourgeois literary public sphere," the literary self-consciousness of private persons:

> Even before the control over the public sphere by public authority was contested and finally wrested away by the critical reasoning of private persons on political issues, there evolved under its cover a public sphere in apolitical form –the literary precursor of the public sphere operative in the political domain. It provided

the training ground for a critical public reflection still preoccupied with itself –a process of self-clarification of private people focusing on the genuine experiences of their novel privateness. [. . .] The public sphere in the world of letters was not, of course, autochthonously bourgeois; it preserved a certain continuity with the publicity involved in the representation enacted at the prince's court. The bourgeois avant-garde of the educated middle class learned the art of critical-rational public debate through its contact with the "elegant world." This courtly-noble society, to the extent that the modern state apparatus became independent from the monarch's personal sphere, naturally separated itself, in turn, more and more from the court and became its counterpoise in the town. (Habermas 29-30)

The "literary public sphere" communicates the differentiated sensibility of educated people among private persons. Habermas points to the intimate relations between the seigniorial society (Elias's "courtly society") and the emerging literary space of the bourgeoisie. I have mentioned that these relations are the material basis of the transition from the figure of courtier in the Renaissance to Gracián's hero in the Baroque, a transition that takes place within the culture of a refined and noble "conversation" among citizens.

Moreover, the "literary" conversation further expands into a public communication a drive for recognition and self-affirmation. The Prologue of *Lazarillo* clearly states this individually-oriented drive in 1554:

> dice Plinio que no hay libro por malo que sea que no tenga alguna cosa buena. [. . .] Y esto, para que ninguna cosa se debría romper ni echar a mal, si muy detestable no fuese, sino que a todos se comunicase, mayormente siendo sin perjuicio y pudiendo sacar della algún fruto. Porque si así no fuese, muy pocos escribirían para uno solo, pues no se hace sin trabajo, y quieren, ya que lo pasan, ser recompensados no con dineros, mas con que vean y lean sus obras, y, si hay de qué, se las alaben. (*Lazarillo* 93)

> (Pliny says that there is no book, even the worst one, that lacks something good [. . .] This is why nothing should be discarded, unless really detestable, but rather everything must be communicated to all, particularly if it is without damage and when it can bear some fruit. Otherwise very few would write only for oneself

since it is not done without effort, and because of that they want to be rewarded not with money, but with seeing and reading their works and, if there is a reason, with praising them.)

A century after this early manifestation of a writer's self-consciousness, Gracián conceives writing as a distinctive accomplishment of a higher life that reaches above the experience of vulgarity: "estos hombres (que van a morir) o son insignes o vulgares: si famosos, nunca mueren; si comunes, más que mueran." (*Criticón* III, 289) (these men [about to die] are either illustrious or vulgar: if they are famous they will never die; if they are ordinary, they better die).[8]

The world of the intellect and literary fame is a particular area of the world of mundane affairs that qualifies persons above the rest of the *vulgo*. The verbal sophistication that the person must display in his social conduct is the material ground for the aesthetic complexity and intended "obscurity" of the Baroque:

> The question of difficulty is at once an aesthetic and an ethical matter. The cultivation of obscurity can be rewarding for the creator and for the consumer; it can be, for both, mind expanding. The exercises in wit, in rhetoric, and in linguistic invention challenge the writer to explore subtleties of thought and of expression, which the reader must attempt to match, and to comprehend. [. . .] Baltasar Gracián and others document and dissect the process in their anatomies of wit. Mental sharpness and ingenuity serve as guidelines and as goals of the undertaking. (Friedman, "Ideologies of Discourse..." 56)

Literature exemplifies a world of competing actors that play linguistically within confusing expressions and difficult meaning. Gracián's paradoxes are expressions of a world of writing that changes and defines its scope along the verbal struggle of literary actors. Writing reflects these accomplishments of culture, which Gracián seems to conceive as the verbal-literary space that mediates the intellectual world and the secular intentions of competing actors. As a cultural event, life is then the intellectual development of

---

[8] The extraordinary numbers of books is, for Gracián, another symptom of a vulgar life. (Cf. *Criticón* III, 304). This is so because books multiply for the many something that is only for the few, the select persons.

a person who grows between subjective intentions and a complex external conduct.

Furthermore, life is an intellectual endeavor. It is the actualization of the mind's effort to emulate the glories of the past in the concrete activity of an interpersonal struggle to acquire a higher position in the world of words. Life and the process of living is the object of culture and, in particular, of writing as the representation of the complex meaning of social exchanges.

CHAPTER 4

A MERCANTILE CONSCIOUSNESS. *GUZMÁN DE ALFARACHE* AND GRACIÁN ON WEALTH

THE bourgeoisie expands the fight for commerce into a general commitment with the wealth of society. In this context, the demands of political economists express an ideological alliance between the values of commerce and a "reform" of poverty.

The life of a person who writes on the means to reconcile religious values with a social conduct aimed at acquiring a profit over other people represents, in my view, the cultural discourse of a mercantile consciousness. Guzmán's inner dialogue illustrates how the economic consciousness of the merchant class increases the demands for a more rationalistic conception of spirituality. In this context, Guzmán constructs a duality between faith and wealth with the purpose of showing their integration in his "self."

The conversion of the *pícaro* responds to a demand for a rationalization (a calculation) of wealth and faith in the life of those searching to avoid the evils of both poverty and corrupting idleness. Alemán's attack on social diseases responds directly to the need of the merchant class to build a differentiated area of social exchange where lower classes looking for an economic integration would participate. The different roles of the *pícaro*, his career from abundance to poverty, his brief moments of luxury and idleness, and his unwilling subordination to nobility, all show a broader dialogue on the moral grounds for a productive economic conduct.

In the following pages, I argue that some literary texts and above all Gracián's approach to social exchange conceptualize the topic of appearances in terms of an intellectual richness that produces more wealth. The intentions of the actors of this exchange create a world of appearances within which people pursue their interests. The meaning of these appearances is a value that individuals may play with in their competition and self-affirmation against and over others. The uncertainty of appearances and the hidden intention of the people demand a strategy both in action and in language.

A social arena conceived as the result of the production of intentional appearances calls for the development of actors whose interests would be better designed if they managed to perceive the "true" value of somebody else. The *pícaro* introduces an economic meaning to certain aristocratic and religious values in order to unveil the place of a monetary society crossing through the boundaries of the privileges of the seigniorial society.

Gracián provides an intellectualization of this process with his depiction of an increase or decrease of the person's intellectual capital. He portrays social exchanges in their double aspect of a public conduct and verbal confrontations. I believe that from the symbolic use of the term *caudal* to the description of a specific social space where knowledge and language are instruments to assess the value of appearances, Gracián realizes the synthesis of a mercantile consciousness.

I begin by analyzing *caudal*, a word that in some cases means economic wealth and in others intellectual disposition, skills and talents. By means of irony, parody and rhetoric, many considerations about religion, love and the function of knowledge in the evaluation of other individuals, become symbolic dimensions of wealth. My analysis hopes to serve as a heuristic device to point to the representation of wealth in the guise of cultural values, that is in values linked to religious ideas, signs of social distinction and intellectual capacity.

At the beginning of the seventeenth century, Mateo Alemán's Guzmán and López de Úbeda's Justina –the female rogue in *La pícara Justina*– offer with the term *caudal* an economic metaphor of the redemption of God and of the sensuality of love, respectively. Some years later María de Zayas implies, moreover, analogous equivalencies between poetic creativity and the means for producing wealth. In Gracián, I shall show that *caudal* blends both economic and rhetorical elements in the description of the capacity to secure the self amid permanent confrontation.

To be sure, these are contradictory, pragmatic, and at times immoral attitudes; they can also be read as an indictment of character, particularly that of the *pícaros*. However, I am concerned with a conceptualization of social life that entails a symbolic capitalization of ideas and beliefs. By a metaphorical movement between economic referents and symbolic definitions, the activity of the mind *enriches* an inner dimension of the self. Gracián portrays this inner dimension as always being on guard and in need of constant reinforcement.

Indeed, both Guzmán and Justina use *caudal* to connote economic values in transcendent ideas. Ironically or sarcastically, they seem to say that the higher the idea, the greater the value one can extract from it. While Justina wants to cash in on the value of love for wealth, Guzmán strives for divine credit to buy the Christian grace.

In both Zayas's and Gracián's use of *caudal*, economic wealth is a metaphor for intellectual and linguistic qualities. Gracián seems also to be pointing at an additional, economic signification of cultural skills, a cultural or symbolic capital that the individual acquires in order to maintain or to reach a social standing.[1]

The following analysis reinforces the idea that the economic coloring of Golden Age texts is more than a literary game. Economic values are refigured in a variety of fields of signification. With *caudal* Mateo Alemán translates an economic meaning into a religious one; in Gracián the term expresses an extreme consciousness of the equivalencies between cultural objects and tools —such as proper language, knowledge and mental attributes— on the one hand, and wealth on the other. He does not reduce the former to the latter; rather he describes their symbolic equivalencies within the processes of a secular self.

The Wealth of God

Guzmán says that when he was a galley-prisoner with no prospect of liberation, he reflected upon the course of his life. Peter Dunn rightly considers this episode to be a "moment of self-recognition, (from) there unwinds the long self-exploration in the narra-

---

[1] I follow Bourdieu's characterization of this symbolic or cultural capital. In general terms, it is the field of cultural, aesthetic and symbolic objects through which and by possessing them the individual acquires a distinctive value in a class-society, where the access to those objects are economically conditioned. See bibliography.

tive discourse." (Dunn 188) This self-recognition represents a major turning point in the process of becoming a reformed person because Guzmán reaches at that time a *new* understanding of both his own life and the intellectual instruments to analyze it.

Alemán gives us here an inner dialogue in a religious language that, however, transfigures its constitutive categories to become a discourse on mercantile values. Economic instability has marked Guzmán's life and he has witnessed moral demands placed in a society where people act in order to possess wealth. He wants to find coherence and a rational justification to balance the seemingly contradicting realms of economic need and spiritual fulfillment.

The thing that may move us is, indeed, his sincerity; however, the issue to ask about is his veracity. His discourse intends to find the unifying trend of all the different aspects of his ideas and experiences. In his confession, Guzmán recognizes this trend in his pursuit of *empleo* –an occupation that provides means of subsistence and monetary enrichment. Furthermore, he recognizes that his whole life has been driven by the logic of this pursuit and by the related consequences of a religious cynicism.

The more profound problem for Guzmán is to obtain assurances that a turning point in his employment will also be an expression of the coherence of his own life. It is at this point where we can read an interpretation of the term *caudal* in which the religious impulse emerges out of a quantifiable field of economic affairs. It becomes an instrument for thinking spiritual concerns in a mercantile fashion.

Guzmán says at this moment:

> Buscaste caudal para hacer empleo: búscalo agora y hazlo de manera que puedas comprar la bienaventuranza. Esos trabajos, eso que padeces y cuidado que tomas en servir a ese tu amo, ponlo a la cuenta de Dios. Hazle cargo aun de aquello que has de perder y recebirálo por su cuenta, bajándolo de la mala tuya. Con eso puedes comprar la gracia [...] Sírvelo con un suspiro, con una lágrima, con un dolor de corazón, pesándote de haberle ofendido. Que dándosele a él, juntará tu caudal con el suyo y, haciéndolo de infinito precio, gozarás de vida eterna. (*Guzmán de Alfarache* 890)

> (You looked for wealth as an employment: look for it again but in a way that you can buy salvation. These efforts, your suffering

and the care that you take to serve your lord, put it on God's account. Charge him even what you will lose and he will receive it as his own taking it off yours. Then you can buy the grace [. . .] Serve to him with a sigh, with a tear, with your heart's pain, being sorry for having offended him. Give it to him and he will combine your wealth with his, and with an infinite price you will enjoy eternal life.)

Guzmán says to himself that he may buy the grace with an investment of his *caudal* in God's *caudal*, in which even bad actions in the past and failures in the future become capitalized. Moreover, the economic expression implies a further transformation of his actions with the intention of extracting an additional signification from his employment, from his social being.[2]

Guzmán has been always after *caudal*. He must now look for *caudal* in a broader sense, one that includes his own spirituality. This emerging sense of cultural capital encompasses a symbolic feature that Guzmán may concretize by means of some external signs. These signs are the embodiment of the economic needs of his life.

This capital intervenes as a credit within the mental activity of religious meditation. Notions of spiritual fulfillment may function in fashion similar to the desire for money that Guzmán knows so well. Guzmán seems to ponder the possibility that the future moment of redemption might resemble the instant of acquiring cash. This redemption will pay his social and religious debt and will liberate him from prison, preparing his soul for eternal life.

Redemption through cash has been the motivation behind Guzmán's drive for social improvement. His life has become a narrative that provides meaning to a state of want and economic frustration. Analyzing the episode of the Milanese merchant when Guzmán gets away with a fraud, Nina Davis accurately saw that an awareness of the value of language permitted Guzmán to exchange words for money (*Autobiography as 'Burla'*... 116). Through his conversion, Guzmán understands the different chapters of his life

---

[2] "[Guzmán] ha hecho de la convivencia un libro mayor en el que escrupulosamente anota las partidas económicas y espirituales, como corresponde a quien quiere estar a buenas con Dios y con los hombres." (Montalvo 132) ([Guzmán] has transformed social relationship into an accounting book where he scrupulously annotates economic and spiritual entries, as the proper thing for he who wants to be in God's favor and in men's favor.)

as following a plot that gives meaning to his soul; a plot whose analogy is the realization of monetary benefits. These benefits are necessarily dependent on intellectual skills that enable him to do the conversion.

Guzmán's realization of the benefits of the spiritual-mental world represents his purpose in life. A purpose included, we may assume, in God's design and therefore it is a purpose of "infinite price," with the never-ending possibility of increasing its value. His meditation allows him to establish a distance between his daily strive for material acquisition, on the one hand, and his growth as a social and a psychological being, on the other.

This meditation merges several previous digressions. After having said that "no hay otra cordura ni otra ciencia en el mundo, sino mucho tener y más tener; lo que aquesto no fuere, no corre" (there is no other wisdom and science in the world but to possess more and more; beside that, nothing counts) Guzmán says that nobody cares about the inner meaning of the soul:

> No te darán silla ni lado cuando te vieren desplumado, aunque te vean revestido de virtudes y ciencia. Ni se hace ya caso de los tales. Empero, si bien representares, aunque seas un muladar, como estés cubierto de yerba, se vendrán a recrear en ti [...] Cuando fueres alquimia, eso que reluciere de ti, eso será venerado. Ya no se juzgan almas ni más de aquello que ven los ojos. Ninguno se pone a considerar lo que sabes, sino lo que tienes; no tu virtud, sino la de tu bolsa; y de tu bolsa no lo que tienes, sino lo que gastas. (*Guzmán de Alfarache*, 680)

> (They will not give you a chair or company if they see you broke, even if they see you dressed with virtues and science. They do not care about them anymore. However, if your representation is good, even if you are a garbage dump but covered with grass they will come to play with you [. . .] If you were alchemy, they will revere whatever shines in you. They do not judge souls anymore or anything beyond what eyes can see. Nobody considers what you know, but what you have; not your virtue, but your purse; not how much you have in it, but how much you spend.)

People care, says Guzmán, about what they can see. Nobody considers knowledge to be worth anything anymore. The only important thing seems to be the "virtue of your purse." This is a very ironic virtue since it shines but evaporates as soon as it is lit. Guzmán says that the value of the soul has been transferred to the act of possessing and, particularly, to the flow of money in exchange. In other words, he makes also the relevant comment that people pay more attention to that flow than to the actual ownership of it. He is talking about what much scholarship has traditionally called the question of "appearances," in the sense of the external circumstances of the person as opposed to its "real" attributes.

In fact, Guzmán is considering here the question of appearances though not in the sense of a pure externality of "things," but as expressions and demands of hierarchies according to money. These expressions might be morally wrong, but they function to valorize the social standing of the person. A valorization emerging from spending money seems to point to a predominance of the exchange and the circulation of wealth over its actual production. This is certainly the situation of any market within an emerging and still marginal bourgeois society, and it clearly describes the particular conditions of the Castilian economy, as I tried to show in the first chapter. Moreover, Guzmán's spiritual mercantilism advances a conceptualization of ideas in economic and, specifically, monetary terms.

The meaning of these ideas is not something isolated from the monetary discourse, or is the money-talk merely a form of a "deeper" content. In his investigation on the transitions from the medieval to a modern literary economy, Marc Shell has expressed very well this necessary sympathy between language and money:

> [That] money and language are complementary or competing systems of tropic production and exchange suggests that money not only is one theme, metaphoric content, or "root metaphor" in some works of language, but also participates actively in all [. . .] The monetary information of thought, unlike its content, cannot be eradicated from discourse without changing thought itself, within whose tropes and processes the language of wares is an ineradicable participant. (Shell 180)

Guzmán's mercantile conversion is, in fact, the outcome of a meditation *through language* on the value of the signs of both wealth and salvation. As he recounts his own life in mercantile terms, the structure of this movement of transformation discovers a mechanics that provides the values of credit and cash through image and signification.

Emerging as a result of expenditures, appearances permit to advance in the race for the accumulation of money. Being an activity in the sphere of business, the external attributes configure an additional asset since "la ostentación es parte de caudal, por lo que al crédito importa." (762) (Ostentation is part of wealth because it influences the credit.)

This credit reflects both a moral reputation and the economic trust placed in one's possibility of expenditure. It is an economic activity working in the moral sphere, transforming it in an interest-oriented field of signification. His notion of a social and moral reputation refers to a bourgeois attribute, the one a decent individual must convince people he has. In this sense, he sees that both meanings of credit –the moral and the economic– blend in the social representation of his spiritual needs.

THE WEALTH OF LOVE

The representation of a world ruled by deception and unrestricted drives from independence and wealth acquires an extreme view in the literature of the *pícaras*. This is because the *pícara* represents –probably even more than her male counterpart– a profound break with the moral and social expectations of the seigniorial hierarchy. As Peter Dunn has seen, the female rogue:

> may entice male victims, but she is independent of their social roles. Indeed, since she is most typically a confidence trickster, she operates by exploiting automatic masculine expectations concerning her sexuality, her need for male protection, and so forth and then frustrating them. (Dunn 248)

Individual disengagement from traditional social roles is one of the major consequences of the emergence of a civil society; so is also the self-reflective search for improvement through the acquisition of an economic well being. These *pícaras* transform legitimate norms and conventions governing the attainment of these goals to such an extent that the meaning of these conventions suffers a radical and threatening alteration.

Justina ascribes an economic value to the game of love. She parodies the language and conventions of courtly love, a tradition that in seventeenth century Spain reinforced traditional conceptions of women in the circles of higher classes.[3] Justina, however, seems to question these conceptions by converting her love into an object of exchange. At one point, she decides to get married and have suitors. In order to choose the proper husband Justina evaluates some of the attitudes and strategies that men express when they seek love. She rejects the men who spend their time looking at women standing at the window:

> amor que sale primero a los ojos y a los meneos que a las manos, no creo en él; manos muertas y ojos vivos es imaginación y chimera de amor. Si con este éxtasis de contemplación tuvieran obras realengas, era entrar por camino real, mas esotras veredas no las conozco. Reniego del amor, si ese es amor. Creer que en mirar ventanas echa el amor su caudal es creer que sin fundamento pintaron al amor con los ojos vendados [. . .] El amor chapado cierra los ojos y abre los puños, encarcela la lengua y desata la bolsa; en fin, es calentura, que tiene el pulso en las manos. (López de Úbeda 711)

> (I do not believe in love that comes to the eyes and to the gestures of the body before the hands; dead hands and live eyes are an image and a chimera of love. If this ecstasy of contemplation came with royal deeds, it would open a royal road; but I am not familiar with these other shortcuts. If this is love, I deny it. To believe that by looking at windows love offers its wealth, is to believe that they unreasonably painted love blindfolded [. . .] Valuable love closes his eyes and opens his fists, imprisons his tongue and unties his purse; in a word, it is a fever with the palpitation in his hands.)

Justina is speaking of a certain habit, when men walk through the street where a woman lives and look at the window; the woman is supposed to be visible if she accepts one particular man. Justina considers, however, that love is "blind," as the classical image of Cupid suggests, and therefore there is nothing worthy of love in

---

[3] See Cacho, "Los moldes de Pygmalión (sobre los tratados de educación femenina en el Siglo de Oro)."

that game. Love does not show its wealth this way, Justina says; in other words, love does not show an equivalent value for the object it intends to acquire.

Through the whole story, Justin uses a *conceptista* language —a language of puns and conceits— to travel from one layer of meaning to the other. The idea that love comes to the "eyes" clearly refers to the illumination that the beloved woman creates in the man, according to the neo-platonic metaphysics that shaped love poetry in the Renaissance. The next sentence sarcastically confirms her negation. She says that if the ecstasy of contemplation came with royal deeds, it would be possible to enter by the "real" road —meaning both *real* and *royal*, a pun that I will comment on in a few moments.

These ecstasies are both a worldly and a divine feeling of love by which sensual and religious poetry describe their respective objects. However, Justina seems to identify the love that comes to the "eyes" with the love that comes to the *meneos* —bodily movements or shaking. She does not believe in a love of contemplation and the resultant feverish agitation of the senses; she rather wants the love that comes from the *manos* —hands. It would seem that Justina's words here are openly sexual, that she rather prefers an actual feeling to an artificial contemplation and emotion. Indeed, she refers to the sexual aspect of love, but she does so by translating spiritual notions into the realm of acquisition or economic activity.

Justina prefers hands instead of eyes because eyes only produce chimeras; the fever of love —*calentura*— truly palpitates in the hands. She believes that a true lover closes his eyes and offers his palm to give the wealth of his love and to loosen his purse (of coins). In other words, Justina wants to translate the meaning of love from contemplation to the action of actual giving. Edward Friedman has accurately seen that this *pícara* discloses a semiotic-economic system:

> the female presence begins to affect the production of meaning. The semiotic (and economic) system associated with these women [such as Justina] is the body, a visual and sexual commodity. (Friedman, *The Anti-heroine voice...* 73)

In the same mood as Guzmán used to effect his substitution of economic credit for virtue and knowledge, Justina transforms the ideal world of neo-Platonism into commerce of sensuality.[4]

---

[4] This *pícara* continues the literary tradition of *La Celestina* in the drive to ex-

Justina and many other *pícaras* transform love and sexuality into goods to be exchanged for money. Moreover, this transformation entails, like Guzmán's mercantilization of religious wealth, a linguistic refinement. In their search for social advance, they valorize spiritual ideas by economic referents. Guzmán capitalizes God's redemption and Justina, his self-proclaimed fiancée, capitalizes the emotions and desires of love.

Justina says that contemplation is not "real" –neither real or royal. Royal deeds –*obras de realengo*– were instruments for the State to intervene in the matters and finances of the Church or of any other seigniorial or local institution. Contemplation, she says, takes many paths but it does not take the royal path, which is the way to sovereignty and to the State's treasure. Laughing at the idea of contemplation, Justina of course emphasizes her corporeality and sexuality.[5]

She intends to write her body upon an emblematic text on which is drawn a paradoxical figure of spirituality and sex, purity and degradation, love and money.[6]

Justina's *caudal* is openly a *concepto* of naked profitability. Through a playful writing –the whole book is a collection of puns

---

change an economic benefit for ideas and words. According to Maravall, this representation in picaresque literature of greedy women is due to the ideological and social reinforcement of a seigniorial system attempting to block social mobility to any member outside the privileged, male-dominated, classes (see particularly chapter XIII of *La literatura picaresca desde la historia social*). The moral stigmatization of women was also the means to impose a marginalization of ethnic minorities in order to articulate a racial discourse of a pure and authentic Spanish identity (see Perry, "The Politics of Race, Ethnicity and Gender in the Making of the Spanish State"). This discourse served well the patrimonial interests of the rentier classes and the Church, and pervaded the ideological horizon of any group striving to reach economic privileges.

[5] Cf.: "la realidad corporal, voluptuosa y sensual, aunque se vela, no por eso deja de tener una presencia en la narración tan importante, al menos, como la realidad explícita y aparentemente moral." (Rey Hazas 89) (even though the bodily reality –sensual and voluptuous– is veiled, it does not stop of having a presence in the narration, which is at least as important as the explicitly and apparently moral reality).

[6] The visualization of her body through her writing is a consequence, at least partially, of López de Úbeda's *conceptismo*. It is a visualization that plays with the tradition of emblematic literature (see Jones, "Hieroglyphics in *La Pícara Justina*") as well as with a grotesque imagery of the sexual body, in a Bakhtinian sense (see Hoogstraten, *Estructura mítica de la picaresca*, particularly 69-105). Nina Davis observes that the patriarchal encroachment of Justina's body and her figuration within the male pornographic imagination is subverted by the appropriation of the authorial voice. ("Breaking the Barriers: The Birth of López de Úbeda's *Pícara Justina*").

or a *Libro de entretenimiento*– López de Úbeda's literary figure discloses a cultural bridge that crosses from virtue to sexuality: a cultural bridge that is a form of valorization itself. Justina laughs because she knows that this cultural bridge works like money. Joan Ramon Resina, analyzing Cervantes's *La gitanilla* concludes that:

> que el valor de Preciosa se plantee no como un problema de esta mujer sino como un problema de todas las mujeres, sugiere que no es la personalidad ni la individualidad lo que se opone a la impersonalidad del linaje, sino el equivalente universal de la virtud, que tendrá en el dinero confirmación y especificación mundanas. (Resina 281)

> (depicting Preciosa's value not as a problem of this woman, but as a problem of every women suggests that what is opposing the impersonal lineage is not personality or individuality, but the universal equivalent of virtue that will have in money its worldly confirmation and particularity.)

Cervantes's character, Preciosa, comes from the "degraded" world of a gypsy community and reaches the center of seigniorial power because her virtue acts as a mechanism of exchange. Justina gives virtue and love the appearances of a mercantile value but, more dramatically or more cynically, she wants to convert that value into real cash –to loosen the purse and open the hand, to embrace the sensuality of touching.[7]

Guzmán and Justina reveal similar conceptions of wealth. They both begin by questioning appearances. They confront the reality of a mercantile world where moral, religious and spiritual values are linguistically expressed in monetary terms; they call *caudal* the relationship among all of these values, and thus arrive at an economic view of intellectual traditions.

These two *pícaros* express this economic view in a more reflective manner than other rogues that follow them. However, this is the view that dominates practically the entire corpus of picaresque narratives. In general, the literature of the *república* –I have been arguing– introduces this view as a symptom of the new social relations

---

[7] Shell offers an interpretation of the technical term "verbal usury" in Shakespeare's *The Merchant of Venice*, by analyzing how the textual working of puns unveils an economic meaning (Shell, 49 ff.).

within civil society. It is not useless to emphasize that, in the threshold of the seventeenth century, this civil society is a marginal sphere within seigniorial power. The perception of threatening conducts and the placement of these conducts as the product of a degraded world, imposes itself in most of the texts on *pícaros*.

In *La hija de Celestina, la Ingeniosa Elena* (1612, 1619) Salas Barbadillo writes a story where the *pícara* is subordinated to the authorial voice of the narrator to demonstrate her evil character. She uses her beauty and her tricks in order to, first seduce a young man, and then rob his rich uncle. She ends by being executed and her body thrown into the river of the city. Several other texts reveal this tension between an aristocratic framework and the description of female protagonists with a sharp and cunning intelligence.[8] In almost all instances, the tension is resolved by means of a moral and physical condemnation of the *pícaras*. As Cruz has rightly concluded:

> The more liberated the protagonist of a female picaresque novel, therefore, the stronger the condemnation by its author of women in general, and the more insistent the warnings of the potential hazards in permitting both 'decent' and 'indecent' women to interact without any differentiation. (Cruz 155)

The submission of the female character to the ideas of the narrator reflects the imposition of the aristocratic ideology over the values of economic drives for individual success and social mobility. Unlike Alemán's *Guzmán*, the degradation that these women inflict in the seigniorial hierarchy is not counterbalanced by a self-reflective justification of the person.

In my view, these narratives –like Quevedo's *Buscón*– fall under the "organicist" literature that Juan Carlos Rodríguez has proposed. In the case of the *pícaras*, the representation of enrichment is fused with criminality and with the centuries-old blame on women and sexuality as the cause of disorder and evil. The aristocratic perspective intervenes in the literature of the *república* precisely with the purpose of re-conducting and judging the ambivalent representation of self-assertion introduced by the increasing monetary circulation along growing spaces of private dealings.

---

[8] The stories that form *Las harpías en Madrid* by Castillo Solórzano is a good example.

Justina's view of *caudal* shows a particular moment of "confusion" and ambivalence, since the text displays the prostitute's cunning intelligence and her satirical comments without any authoritarian voice supervising them. It is only in the prologue where the "author" moralizes against her. She even ends happily married to Guzmán de Alfarache, and finishes her own story with a "good night" to the reader before going to enjoy the "noche de bodas" (weeding night).

The Wealth of the Mind

The literature of the *pícaras* shows some of the extreme dangers of breaking seigniorial spaces. They elaborate on the tradition initiated by *La Celestina*, and in particular by the incorporation of sexuality to linguistic exchanges. The wealth of these women concentrates on their bodies, but also and prominently on their verbal performances. [9] Their words are truly instruments of economic goals, which in turn the texts portray as undermining the orderly meaning of the world.

Justina plays with language to the same degree that she satirizes seigniorial values such as honor, lineage and purity. She transforms these values into money-like means of purchasing a false social identity. As with Guzmán, this (false) identity constitutes a good that may entitle her to aspire to higher privileges and riches. The economic need is always the ultimate referent in the *linguistic* transformation she shameless effects both as a writer of her non-exemplary life and as an actor in countless scenarios of trickery and deception.

María de Zayas, on the contrary, seems to offer an exclusively literary meaning of the term *caudal*, which in my view situates her closer to the full intellectualization of Gracián. In the prologue to her collection of short stories, Zayas supports her right to write and to publish books with a defense of the intellectual capacity of women. She argues that women display less intelligence than men do because women do not have access, as men do, to education and to a proper intellectual training:

---

[9] Jennifer Cooley provides a brilliant analysis of the linguistic performance of marginal characters in her book *Courtiers, Courtesans, Pícaros and Prostitutes*.

las almas ni son hombres ni mujeres; ¿qué razón hay para que ellos sean sabios y presuman que nosotras no podemos serlo? Esto no tiene a mi parecer más respuesta que su impiedad o tiranía en encerrarnos, y no darnos maestros; y así, la verdadera causa de no ser las mujeres doctas no es defecto del caudal, sino falta de la aplicación, porque si en nuestra crianza como nos ponen el cambray en las almohadillas y los dibuxos en el bastidor, nos dieran libros y preceptores, fuéramos tan aptas para los puestos y para las cátedras como los hombres. (Zayas 48)

(souls are not male or female; what is the reason for men to be wise and to presume that we [women] cannot? In my opinion, there is no other reason than their tyranny confining us without teachers; thus, the real reason that women are not cultivated is not a lack of wealth, but a lack of training; if for our upbringing they gave us books and instructors instead of the fabric in the cushions and the patterns in the frame, we would be as capable for the positions and lectureships as men are.)

Zayas argues that knowledge is the very process of acquiring it and that education in itself is the instrument at work within that process. More important, I think, is her distinction between *caudal* and *aplicación*, which may correspond to a distinction between the principles of success and the practice of attaining it. It might be the case, however, that *caudal* in this sentence refers only to economic wealth, since Zayas and the "wise" people were all wealthy or they would not have the time to cultivate their minds. Still, even if that is the case, Zayas understands the intellect as something that increases through practice.

Later in the collection, *caudal* has an unmistakable meaning. A character in one of the novels says that she used to write poetry, which made some men angry:

> hay algunos ignorantes que, como si las mujeres les quitaran el entendimiento por tenerle, se consumen de los aciertos ajenos. ¡Bárbaro, ignorante! si lo sabes hacer [versos], hazlos, que no te roba nadie tu caudal. (Zayas 210)

(some ignorant men, thinking that women who have understanding take it away from them, get angry at the other's goods. Barbaric, ignorant man! If you know how to create (poetry), do it, nobody is stealing your wealth.)

Some men are so ignorant, says the character, that they fear that women with talents are stealing the understanding from them; but the female poet does not rob anybody's wealth, just because she writes poetry. In negative terms, Zayas confirms the translation of meaning from economic to intellectual or creative terms. Even if the character of the novel is accusing men of thinking that women write in order to obtain men's wealth, the text nevertheless introduces a new element into the conception of wealth. It is the wealth of a different kind of goods.

Caudal is the possession of symbolic goods, in the present case the possession of the skills to produce intellectual works. It is a disposition to possess that provides the individual with a mark of distinction. In other words, economic wealth is thought to be equivalent to the wealth of the mind, to the capacity for creativity.

Zayas establishes an even more explicit relationship between monetary wealth and symbolic-poetic wealth in another short story. High class men and women get together to tell love stories and chat over the bad and good aspects of love. Lisis –the main character– seeks to prove that women must abandon love because men want only to deceive them. She tells men:

> ¿qué razón habrá para que entre las grandes riquezas de vuestros heroicos discursos no halle lugar mi pobre jornalejo? Y supuesto que, aunque moneda inferior, es moneda y vale algo, por humilde, no la habéis de pisar; luego si merece tener lugar entre vuestro grueso caudal, ya os vencéis y me hacéis vencedora. (Zayas 315)

> (what is the reason for not letting my poor salary be among the big wealth of your heroic discourses? Although it is a minor coin, it is a coin and it is worth something, you must not despise it; then, if it deserves to have a place in your great wealth, you triumph over yourselves and make me triumph.)

Caudal here is the flow of literary competence and the wealth of poetic discourse. Lisis wants to join this male-dominated wealth with her *jornal* –the payment of a workday– because, though small and humble, her asset is also *moneda* –currency– and has a value.

The poetic wealth is distributed unequally throughout the group. Zayas points out again this hierarchical access to wealth in general, and particularly the differences in the possession of a poetic-literary wealth; in other words, she portrays the social hierarchy according to the capacity to produce, accumulate and realize creative language. In this sense, her explicit economic homology on value of ideas and language expresses a cultural qualification to the literary references of wealth. *Caudal* is not merely wealth; it is also a clear symptom of a symbolic dimension of capital, in which the productive activity of language establishes the value of a social enterprise, in this case the collective enterprise of poetry.

Mateo Alemán had a cultural qualification of *caudal* when, in a letter to his friend involved in the reform of welfare, he writes that he is not wealthy enough to talk about poverty:

> Muchas veces me puse a considerar (O amigo Máximo) y muchas noches, aun cansado de negocios, dejé de pagar el censo a naturaleza, desveládome en el amparo de los pobres, tanto por el bien común cuanto por mi propio interés que, habiendo de tratar su causa, no pudiera excusar la mía. Pero como semejante trato requería más acción y mayor poder, siempre lo temí, viéndome falto del caudal que pide tan alta mercadería y materia tratada de tan doctos varones que, cuando quisiese decir algo, sería reiterar lo que ellos tienen dicho y estampado y a todos es notorio. (in Cros, *Protée et le gueux* 436)

> (Many times I have pondered, my great friend, and many nights, even being tired of my businesses, I did not pay the rent to nature, awake thinking about how to help the poor, because of the common good and because my own interest, since if I wanted to treat its cause I could not avoid my own. However, since such treatment required more action and more power, I always feared it lacking the wealth that such high merchandise asks for, and it has been treated by such wise men that anything I said would be to repeat what they have already said and published and is so well known.)

He finds himself so concerned with the problems of the poor that he even does not pay the rent to nature –sleeping. This is because daily life costs money, of course. Alemán's life is full of businesses –*negocios*– and when he ponders the question of poverty he feels he does not have enough capital –*caudal*– to do business –*tratar*– on such an important commodity –*mercadería*.

There are then clear identifications between a subject of inquiry, the question of poverty as a commodity, on the one hand, and intellectual capacity and economic wealth, on the other. Alemán says that the business of poverty affects the common good as well as his own interests. He fears he has nothing to add to what many wise people have already said about that issue.

Like Zayas' qualification of the wealth of poetic discourse, Alemán offers a cultural meaning of wealth, one that includes intellectual effort as well as the knowledge to analyze and comment on social interaction. Alemán ironically refers to this wealth of discourse in relation to poverty, pointing –like Zayas– to the equivalencies between economic and symbolic expressions of social differences.

The Wealth of Knowledge and the Status of Appearances

Gracián writes on the constitution of the inner value of the self. For him, an artificial and public projection becomes, paradoxically, a necessity for the worldly Christian persona. With *caudal* Gracián perceives a much stronger relationship between the economic and the symbolic levels of growth.

He refers to the wealth of literary capacities, a quality of *ingenio*, as well as to the wealth of a public conduct, the quality of *prudencia*. He attempts to blend the artificial and representational qualities of public conduct together with the skills of literary creation, the production of *conceptos*.[10]

The distinctive feature that Gracián adds to *caudal* is an identification with knowledge. The nature of the self seems dependent on the amount of knowledge the person has in order to protect himself. Gracián says in the *Oráculo*:

---

[10] The *concepto*, Gracián writes, is "un acto del entendimiento que exprime la correspondencia que se halla entre los objetos." –an act of the understanding that extracts the correspondences among objects– (*Agudeza* I, 55). Parker saw that Gracián meant qualities and attributes, as well as physical things (Parker 21). Among all the extensive bibliography on the linguistic-rhetorical aspects of *concepto* Hernández argues that a "didactic consciousness" works in it (Hernández 19); Blanco points that "El concepto funciona pues como un mecanismo formal que produce la impresión de algo que pensar." (Blanco 34) (The *concepto* works as a formal mechanism that produces the impression of thinking of something).

"*Incomprensibilidad de caudal.* Excuse el varón atento sondearle el fondo, ya al saber, ya al valer, si quiere que le veneren todos: permítase al conocimiento, no a la comprensión. Nadie le averigüe los términos de la capacidad, por el peligro evidente del desengaño. Nunca dé lugar a que alguno le alcance todo: mayores afectos de veneración causa la opinión y duda de adónde llega el caudal de cada uno que la evidencia de él, por grande que fuere." (*Oráculo manual* 172)

(*An incomprehensible wealth.* The alert man must avoid having the bottom tested, in terms of knowledge and in terms or value, if he wants everyone to revere him: one may allow himself to be known but not to be comprehended. Nobody must learn the limits of his volume, because of the obvious danger if disappointed. He must never permit that somebody comprehend it all: greater feelings of veneration are motivated by the opinion and doubt of how far one's wealth goes than the proof of it, no matter how big it actually is.)

Caudal is an intimate sphere that produces a value of distinction. It is the source of a conceptual power or a wealth of rhetorical attributes. At the beginning of *El héroe*, Gracián describes a state of human relations where the hero is capable of converting linguistic tools into means of aggression and defense:

Arguye eminencia de caudal penetrar toda voluntad ajena, y concluye superioridad saber celar la propia. (*El héroe*, 9)

[To know how to penetrate the other's will is the discourse of a superior wealth; to know how to defend one's will is its highest conclusion.]

Rhetorical aspects –"arguments" and "conclusions"– indicate a proper linguistic dimension in which to assert one's will by subjugating and triumph over other's. Success in these enterprises demonstrates the possession of a wealth to master a sphere of discursive confrontation. By articulating the mechanisms of metaphorical imagination with the goals of social exchange, Gracián converts material acquisition into language.[11]

---

[11] In a similar vein, Malcolm Read sees that "Commercial thinking penetrates into the very core of Gracián's being [..] Human virtues are remodeled according to commercial values, from which it is but a short step to the denigration of the intellectual in favor of the more practical man." ("Saving Appearances..." 104-5)

The value of the linguistic performance emerges in the circulation of discourse, as an expression of a competition for privileges. Language and monetary wealth coincide, then, in their functional relationship with the production of a profit, which for Gracián results in the imposition of the self. Moreover, the self maintains an even closer homology with economic growth in the sense that his actualization in exchange resembles the use of wealth as the means for acquiring more wealth.

Thus, he arrives at an intimate relationship between self and knowledge where the self emerges from the power of conceptualization and knowledge becomes a set of instruments for mapping the battlefield of society. For it is one's self, Gracián argues, which is at stake at every social exchange and which the person must nourish through life. Knowledge is, to Gracián, the means for social survival:

> *Tener un punto de negociante.* No todo sea especulación, haya también acción. Los muy sabios son fáciles de engañar, porque, aunque saben lo extraordinario, ignoran lo ordinario del vivir, que es más preciso [. . .] ¿De qué sirve el saber si no es práctico? Y el saber vivir es hoy el verdadero saber. (*Oráculo manual* 212-213)

> (*Have the touch of a businessman.* Not everything ought to be speculation, action is also needed. The wisest men are easily deceived because though they know extraordinary things they ignore the routine of life that is more precise [. . .] What is the purpose of knowledge if it is not practical? To know how to live is today the true knowledge.)

True knowledge is, Gracián says, the knowledge of how to live. One must be like a businessman –*negociante*– in order to deal with other people in everyday life. The fundamental need for this practical knowledge arises out of the vital function it has in the constitution of the persona, which in turns depends on the "amount", depth and strength of interiority. In this sense, the person lives "en un mundo que sólo va a tener justificación si existen en él individuos que se sobrepongan." (Asún X) (in a world only justified if there are individuals capable of triumph).

The defense of oneself requires a rationalization of social dealings. Gracián expresses this rationalization by conflating conduct in the pursuit of success with the knowledge of other people's intentions and desires. This type of knowledge becomes, reciprocally, a wealth invested to acquire somebody else's inner wealth:

> Si todo exceso en secreto lo es en caudal, sacramentar una voluntad será soberanía. Son los achaques de la voluntad desmayos de la reputación; y si se declaran, muere comúnmente. (*El héroe* 8)

> (Excess in secret is also in wealth, so sealing the will is sovereignty. Will's ailments are the reputation's fainting; if they are declared, it dies ordinarily.)

Appearances are, as with Guzmán, an integral component of the credit the individual earns for future actions. In this regard, appearances are not disposable superficialities but shields for the proper protection of the self. Excess and lack of prudence on a variety of issues are potential targets of the intentions of the other people who seek to nourish the growth of their own selves.

Yet, this gesture of perfectibility, this drive to excel and to become a hero is grounded on the conviction that the growth of the self has to be accomplished in radical solitude and in an inhospitable world. Maravall considered that Gracián intended to "organizar el comportamiento recíproco de los individuos, incomunicables como mónadas." ("Antropología y política..." 367) (organize the mutual conduct of individuals that are isolated like monads). Forcione sees in this self "una entidad a la que se le confiere el ser sólo por la contemplación de otros que observan su actuación." ("La disociación cósmica..." 449) (an entity that receives his being only in the contemplation by others observing his conduct). The contemplation of the other becomes an instrument of social aggression and the basis of a relationship between Machiavellian-style politics and the productive dimension of language. In this sense, the knowledge that emerges from a rationalization of the social experience of the intellectual and bureaucratic elite becomes a cultural capital that furthers the social growth of the self.

The importance of imagination in the constitution of ideas on social reality is not, in my view, an indication that "access to the real requires that we relinquish the control of the rational mind." (Read, *The Birth and Death of Language* 207). On the contrary, it can be argued that Gracián's fusion of prudent and poetic qualities in the construction of a hero involves the submission of imagination to the demands of a rational self. Imagination and political morality become inter-related and both needed in the person's life-long process of inquiry. [12] This is so because knowledge of oneself begins with an explanation regarding the other, insofar the other is the target of the self's politics:

> "Vívese lo más de información, es lo menos lo que vemos: vivimos de fe ajena [...] La verdad ordinariamente se ve, extravagantemente se oye; raras veces llega en su elemento puro, y menos cuando viene de lejos; siempre trae algo de mixta, de los afectos por donde pasa [...] Es menester toda la atención en este punto para descubrir la intención del que tercia, conociendo de antemano de qué pie se movió. Sea la refleja, contraste de lo falto y de lo falso." (*Oráculo manual*, 168)
>
> (We live mostly on information, what we see is less important: we live off the trust of others [...] One sees truth ordinarily, one hears truth eccentrically; it hardly comes in its pure element, much less when it comes from far way; it always brings a mixture of the effects it has passed through [...] All the attention is important in this point in order to discover the player's intention beforehand knowing what step he took. Reflection must be the contrast of the missing and the false.)

The person needs to know in order to live. Knowledge is the substance of life, what everybody intends to increase by acquiring life from the other. The very process of knowing is a struggle where the self must discover the other's intentions. In the quoted paragraph Gracián writes specifically about the "art of prudence," the skill the person must have to survive and increase the potential for mastering social exchange. Moreover, in his treatise on the "art of wit" –*arte de ingenio*– Gracián also describes a similar strategic play of intentions in the way truth discloses its nature:

---

[12] Analyzing the *Oráculo*, Jorge Checa writes: "Al fundir las actividades lingüística y moral, la escritura de Gracián en el *Oráculo* simboliza de forma indirecta las operaciones prudentes estipuladas para la vida cotidiana. En el plano del estilo, el tratado sobresale por un casi obsesivo deslinde del matiz y de la expresión más ceñida; todo ello corresponde a [...] la búsqueda del momento justo para acometer un empeño arriesgado y el hallazgo de la oportunidad." ("*Oráculo manual*: Gracián y el ejercicio de la lectura" 266)

> Abrió los ojos la Verdad, dio desde entonces en andar con artificio, usa de las invenciones, introdúcese por rodeos, vence con estratagemas, pinta lejos lo que está muy cerca, habla de lo presente en lo pasado, propone en aquel sujeto lo que quiere condenar en éste, apunta en uno para dar en otro, deslumbra las pasiones, desmiente los afectos, y, por ingenioso circunloquio, viene siempre a parar en el punto de su intención. (*Agudeza y arte de ingenio* II, 192)

> [Truth opened its eyes; since then, it began to walk with artfulness; it uses inventions, comes by roundabout ways, wins by means of strategies, paints far away what is actually nearby; it speaks about today through the past, proposes something on that subject which it actually condemns on this other, aims at this one to target at that other; it blinds passions, refutes affections and, by an ingenious circumlocution it finally arrives at the matter of its intention.]

The strategy of intentions –in social performance as well as in the way truth finds its way through deceptions– is a conceptual or symbolic field where the person shows its value. This value becomes the sign of his *caudal*, his wealth and his own life. Moreover, this value is his social projection as it is the product of practical knowledge. This practical side is not merely a complement to general knowledge but a necessary "art" of intentions.

Caudal is also formal knowledge:

> Pues sabed que ésas [las universidades] son las oficinas donde se funden los buenos caudales, ahí se forjan los grandes hombres, en esos talleres se desbastan de troncos y de estatuas y se labran los mayores sujetos. (*Criticón* III, 157)

> (So you should know that these universities are offices where good wealth is melted, it is where great men are forged; in these shops the highest subjects are carved and worked out of trunks and statutes.}

Formal knowledge produces wealth in the sense that it produces the highest "subjects." These subjects develop a particular taste for intellectual affairs which, in turn, would serve as the feature of their cultural distinction. Their higher taste for an intellectual "conversation" is an activity that, together with musical and culinary tastes, produce a sense of belonging to a sphere of private sensibilities:

> Y para que fuese el viaje de todas maneras gustoso, iba entreteniéndoles el Inmortal con su sazonada conversación: que no hay rato hoy más entretenido ni más aprovechado que el de un *bel parlar* entre tres o cuatro. Recréase el oído con la suave música, el gusto en un convite; pero el entendimiento, con la erudita y discreta conversación entre tres o cuatro amigos entendidos, y no más, porque en pasando de ahí, es bulla y confusión. De modo que es la dulce conversación banquete del entendimiento, manjar del alma, desahogo del corazón, logro del saber, vida de la amistad y empleo mayor del hombre. (*Criticón* III, 296)

> (To make the trip pleasant, the Immortal entertained them with his tasteful conversation: today there is no time more pleasant and fruitful that a *bel parlar* between three or four. The ears enjoy tender music, the taste enjoys an invitation; the understanding, however, requires an erudite and discreet conversation between three or four cultivated friends, no more because beyond that it is a noise and a confusion. Then, sweet conversation is a feast of the understanding, fine food for the soul, relief for the heart, accomplishment of knowledge, life of friendship and the highest employment of man.)

The refined pleasures of persons are the outcome of a process of selection determined by the awareness that a cultural sphere decisively influences the social structure of people. Persons are individuals of culture, people who in their privacy have the tools to value and discriminate among the products that their souls enjoy.

This discrimination has a value also because it permits the person to inquire into the conditions of his social projections and the significance of a literary world. Literature, or the circuit of writing and reading, is the process through which these select individuals may confront a "circumstantial" reality:

> Ya os dije que todo cuanto hay en el mundo pasa en cifra: el bueno, el malo, el ignorante y el sabio [. . .] Las más de las cosas no son las que se leen: ya no hay que entender pan por pan, sino por tierra, ni vino por vino, sino por agua, que hasta los elementos están cifrados en los elementos: ¡qué serán los hombres! Donde pensaréis que hay sustancia, todo es circunstancia, y lo

que parece más sólido es más hueco, y toda cosa hueca, vacía. (*Criticón* III, 98)

(I already told you that everything in the world exists in cipher: the good, the bad, the ignorant and the wise man [. . .] Most of the things are not what you read in them: we cannot anymore understand bread as bread but as dirt, or wine as wine but as water, because even the elements are ciphered in the elements: what about men! Where you think there is substance everything is circumstantial; and what seems to be more solid is hollow and every hollow thing is empty.)

What are these circumstances? They are something close to Descartes's appearances, the way the self perceives the sensible world. Gracián's concern with appearances is also the result of an inquiry on truth and on the status of vision and the senses.[13] His description of appearances resembles the rationalist suspicion regarding the contents of a sensible world that need to be put in doubt before reaching a verdict on its truthfulness. Furthermore, Gracián observes as Descartes does at the beginning of his *Method*, that people do not provide any help in the search for a solid foundation on the status of any opinion and any statement concerning reality. On the contrary, their statements further confuse him and would even seem to do so intentionally.

In Gracián a circumstantial reality refers specifically to the human exchanges of his contemporary society. The practical lesson would be that the person must live with the sense of artificiality and "deception," and try to make use of profitable options. The pessimism of his worldview is rather a particular mixture of rationalist notions and a pragmatical conception of the social act in terms of a process of self-affirmation and success.

The learned person, the person of books, is better prepared to play in social exchanges because Gracián conceives cultural production as the way the intellectual heritage becomes the property of the few select individuals:

---

[13] Maravall maintained that the privilege of 'vision' over 'listening' is one of the major features of the political manipulation of culture in the Baroque. Visual arts joined the spectacles of theater, parades and public festivities in capturing the attention of people in order to provide a conservative message (see *La cultura del Barroco*, particularly 495-524).

> Créeme –decía el enano– que todo pasa en imagen, y aun en imaginación, en esta vida: hasta esa casa del saber toda ella es apariencia [. . .] no hay otro saber sino el que se halla en los inmortales caracteres de los libros: ahí la has de buscar y aprender. (*Criticón* II, 142-143)

> (Believe me –said the dwarf– that in this life everything happens in images and even imagination: even that house of learning is all an appearance [. . .] There is not another knowledge but the one in the immortal letters of the books: there you have to look for and learn.)

Letters in books bear the immortal substance of knowledge, the true reality of human interaction. Images and imagination are, on the contrary, the world of appearances, the world of the senses and fanciful ideas. The substance of reality must be read and decoded:

> La dificultad la hallo yo en leer y entender lo que está de tejas abajo, porque como todo ande en cifra y los humanos corazones estén tan sellados e inescrutables, asegúroos que el mejor lector se pierde. Y otra cosa, que si no lleváis bien estudiada y bien sabida la contracifra de todo, os habréis de hallar perdidos, sin acertar a leer palabra ni conocer letra, ni un rasgo ni una tilde. (*Criticón* III, 96)

> (What I find difficult is reading and understanding the secular world, because since everything is ciphered and human hearts are sealed and inscrutable, I assure you that the best reader gets lost. Something else: if you do not have the lesson well studied and the counter-cipher of everything well learnt, you will get lost, unable to read and recognize any letter, stroke or tilde.)

Ciphers are the language of social reality. They are condensations of meaning that require the sophisticated skills of reading in order to walk through the world –*de tejas abajo*. Human hearts seal their intentions and feelings beyond the reach of knowledge. The learned person is actually a reader of social phenomena who interrogates the language of appearances with the instruments of intellectual work.

The reading of social exchanges has the purpose of enhancing the position of the person according to his interests. The knowledge attained is, then, a knowledge of how other readings affect the very configuration of the social space, since this space is nothing else that the outcome of intentional misreading.

One must be alert, Gracián says, of the deceitful nature of people, their unreliable statements and their hidden thoughts: "hombres de ensenadas, de reflejas y segundas intenciones, de trato nada liso, sino doblado." (*Criticón* III, 147) (men of coves, reflections and second intentions, with a crooked and double conduct). People act in a crooked way, an idea that Gracián portrays by the words plain and doubled: people act with a double sense.

The proper meaning, the single and straight identification of one act or idea with one meaning, always eludes us. In other words, the ciphered language of social exchange responds to the relative status of the value of this exchange, to its changing faces and vaporous circulation. Checa has observed an "arbitrary status" in this language:

> the potentially infinite number of Gracián's *cifras*, together with their arbitrary status, signals how moral discourse chooses and defines its interests following a dynamic point of view, which is always prone to readjustment. (Checa, "Gracián and the Ciphers of the World" 182-183)

Processes of social exchange are disengaged of universally accepted signification. Since verbal and intellectual skills are instruments of the person's strategy, these processes manifest a relative status regarding their truth. They are the outcome of strategies with multiple intentions. The person, then, must be a reader of these intentions, which are devoid of truth but which are the very constitution of meaning in the realm of social values.

The apparent meaning is the instrument of somebody else's self-affirmation. The meaning behind and secluded is the target of the actor's reflection –*refleja* in Gracián's vocabulary. The target is to unveil that "second" meaning and reach the "heart" of the other actors. The whole social exchange, for Gracián, has this purpose of fighting against apparent meanings in order to get into the true value of other people. In this context, *reflejas* are reflective moves that select and exceptional *ingenios* –intellects– do in practical conduct as well as in their inquiry on the conduct of the others:

> Así como el obrar con artificio y con refleja nace de ventaja de ingenio, así el descubrir ese artificio, y el notarlo, es sutileza doblada. (*Agudeza* I, 256)
>
> (In the same way that to act with ability and reflection comes from an eminent intelligence, to discover this ability and to notice it is a double subtlety.)

Agudeza y arte de ingenio is a treatise on rhetoric and preceptive poetics. Even in this context, Gracián makes clear the social relevance of intellectual work and, more specifically, the correspondences between a strategy of intentions in social exchanges and a strategy of interpretation of poetic forms. These correspondences further confirm the intimate relation that intellectual works have with the sphere of a symbolic wealth by which the person capitalizes on the intentional creation of appearances.

CONCLUSION

THIS study has argued that an early bourgeois literature emerges in the Spanish Golden Age. This literature begins by representing an increasing awareness of the autonomy of economic needs and the search for individual wealth as a fictional counterpart of the developments carried on by early political economists. I have proposed to call this representation the literature of the *república*, because with this term some of these economists and jurists seem to point to a conceptualization of a civil society, or a society of economic exchanges.

Economic needs and the status of wealth informs particularly picaresque narratives, although it is only with *Lazarillo de Tormes* and *Guzmán de Alfarache* where a proper bourgeois literary sensibility emerges through the representation of the "person." Lázaro's private person and radical affirmation of his own value, and Guzmán's mercantile conceptions of religious and aristocratic beliefs attempted to fictionalize the individual and social circumstances of poverty, and the obstacles to social improvement and enrichment.

Moreover, Mateo Alemán's *pícaro* acquires a definite characterization of a writer that evaluates his life along the conflicts between the seigniorial power and the horizon of a still marginal bourgeois society. His writing becomes the means to articulate a mercantile consciousness that shows an uncompromising denunciation of a structure of privileges, and an intimate search for a renovated Christian virtue.

Along the economic and political crises of the first half of the seventeenth century and the strengthening of Absolutism the literature of the *república* displays the ideological reaction of the seigniorial hierarchy. The questions of self-affirmation and individual enrichment are fictionalized as symptoms of a degraded world and examples of threats to the privileged groups. Many picaresque stories, if not all, follow this reaction.

Alemán's literary meditation on wealth, however, has a paradigmatic continuation in the texts of Baltasar Gracián, where sophisticated intellectual and linguistic capacities serve the purposes of select people that strive to achieve a high level of cultural distinction. A world now pervaded by the interplay of multiple intentions and the precarious state of truth in human exchanges requires exceptional persons capable of counteracting with verbal virtuosity and intellectual sharpness. In this way, Gracián's representation of the profitability of appearances is a warning of the profound transformations at the heart of the aristocratic system.

BIBLIOGRAPHY

Abellán, José Luis. "Baltasar Gracián, máxima conciencia filosófica del Barroco." *Aporía* 3.10 (1980): 49-69.
Alemán, Mateo. *Guzmán de Alfarache.* Ed. Francisco Rico. Barcelona: Planeta, 1983.
Althusser, Louis. *Machiavelli and Us.* Transl. by Gregory Elliot. London: Verso, 1999.
Artola, Miguel. *La Hacienda del Antiguo Régimen.* Madrid: Alianza Editorial, Banco de España, 1982.
Asún, Raquel. "Introducción." Baltasar Gracián, *El héroe. El discreto. Oráculo manual y arte de prudencia.* Ed. Luys Santa Marina. Barcelona: Planeta, 1990. IX-XXXIX.
Atienza Hernández, Ignacio. *Aristocracia, poder y riqueza en la España moderna. La casa de Osuna.* Madrid: Siglo XXI, 1987.
Baeck, Louis. *The Mediterranean Tradition in Economic Thought.* London and New York: Routledge, 1994.
Bataillon, Marcel. *Erasmo y España. Estudios sobre la historia espiritual del siglo XVI.* Transl. by Antonio Alatorre. México: Fondo de Cultura Económica, 1950.
Beverley, John. "El *Lazarillo* y la acumulación originaria." *Del Lazarillo al Sandinismo: Estudios sobre la función ideológica de la literatura española e hispanoamericana.* Minneapolis: The Prisma Institute, 1987. 47-64.
Blanco, Mercedes. "El mecanismo de la ocultación. Análisis de un ejemplo de agudeza." *Criticón* 43 (1988): 13-36.
Bourdieu, Pierre. *Language and Symbolic Power.* Translated by Gino Raymond and Matthew Adamson. Cambridge: Harvard University Press, 1991.
———. *The Logic of Practice.* Translated by Richard Nice. Stanford: Stanford University Press, 1990.
Bouwsma, William J. *The Waning of the Renaissance. 1550-1640.* New Haven: Yale University Press, 2000.
Braudel, Ferdinand. *The Wheels of Commerce.* Volume 2 of *Civilization and Capitalism.* Translation by Sian Reynolds. Berkeley: University of California Press, 1992.
Brett, Annabel. *Liberty, Right and Nature. Individual Rights in Later Scholastic Thought.* Cambridge: Cambridge University Press, 1997.
Brumont, Francis. *Campo y campesinos de Castilla la Vieja en tiempos de Felipe II.* Madrid: Siglo XXI, 1984.
Cacho, María Teresa. "Los moldes de Pygmalión (sobre los tratados de educación femenina en el Siglo de Oro)." *Breve historia feminista de la literatura española*

(en lengua castellana). Coord. Iris M. de Zavala. II *La mujer en la literatura española.* Madrid: Anthropos, Comunidad de Madrid, 1995. 177-213.

Carande, Ramón. *Los caminos del oro y de la plata.* Volume 3 of *Carlos V y sus banqueros.* Madrid: Sociedad de Estudios y Publicaciones, 1967.

Cascardi, Anthony J. *The Subject of Modernity.* Cambridge: Cambridge University Press, 1992.

Castillo, David. "Gracián and the Art of Public Representation." *Rhetoric and Politics. Baltasar Gracián and the New World Order.* Eds. Nicholas Spadaccini and Jenaro Talens. Minneapolis: The University of Minnesota Press, 1997. 191-208.

Castillo Solórzano, Alonso de. *Las harpías en Madrid.* Ed. Pablo Jauralde Pou. Madrid: Castalia, 1985.

Castrillo, Alonso de. *Tractado de República* (1521). Madrid: Instituto de Estudios Políticos, 1958.

Cavillac, Michel. *Pícaros y mercaderes en el Guzmán de Alfarache.* Translation by Juan Azpitarte. Granada: Universidad de Granada, 1994.

——. "La problemática de los pobres en el siglo XVI." Introduction to his edition of *Amparo de pobres* by Cristóbal Pérez de Herrera. Madrid: Espasa-Calpe, 1975. LXXV-CCIV.

Caxa de Leruela, Miguel. *Restauración de la abundancia de España* (c. 1630). Ed. Jean Paul Le Flem. Madrid: Instituto de Estudios Fiscales, 1975.

Cervantes, Miguel de. *El ingenioso hidalgo Don Quijote de la Mancha.* Ed. Luis Andrés Murillo. Madrid: Castalia, 1978. 2 vols.

——. *Novelas ejemplares.* Ed. Harry Sieber. Madrid: Cátedra, 1986. 2 vols.

Checa, Jorge. "Gracián and the Ciphers of the World." *Rhetoric and Politics. Baltasar Gracián and the New World Order.* Eds. Nicholas Spadaccini and Jenaro Talens. Minneapolis: The University of Minnesota Press, 1997. 170-187.

——. "*Oráculo manual*: Gracián y el ejercicio de la lectura." *Hispanic Review* 59.3 (1991): 263-280.

Cohen, Walter. *Drama of a Nation. Public Theater in Renaissance England and Spain.* Ithaca: Cornell University Press, 1985.

Cooley, Jennifer. *Courtiers, Courtesans, Pícaros and Prostitutes: The Art and Artifice of Selling One's Self in Verbal Exchange.* New Orleans: University Press of the South, 2002.

Cortés de Tolosa, Juan. *Lazarillo de Manzanares.* Ed. Giuseppe E. Sansone. Madrid: Espasa-Calpe, 1974.

Covarrubias, Sebastián de. *Tesoro de la Lengua castellana o española* (1611). Ed. Martín de Riquer. Barcelona: Alta Fulla, 1993.

Cros, Edmond. *Mateo Alemán: Introducción a su vida y a su obra.* Salamanca: Anaya, 1971.

——. *Protée et le gueux. Recherches sur les origines et la nature du récit picaresque dans Guzmán de Alfarache.* Paris: Didier, 1967.

Cruz, Anne J. *Discourses of Poverty: Social Reform and the Picaresque Novel in Early Modern Spain.* Toronto: University of Toronto Press, 1999.

Davis, Nina. "Breaking the Barriers: The Birth of López de Úbeda's *Pícara Justina.*" *The Picaresque. Tradition and Displacement.* Ed. Giancarlo Maiorino. Minneapolis: The University of Minnesota Press, 1996. 137-158.

——. *Autobiography as 'Burla' in the* Guzmán de Alfarache. London and Toronto: Associated University Press, 1991.

Descartes, René. *Discourse on the Method of Rightly Conducting the Reason and Seeking Truth in the Sciences.* Transl. by John Veitch. New York: Anchor Books, 1974.

Deyermond, Alan. "Divisiones socio-económicas, nexos sexuales: La sociedad de *Celestina.*" *Celestinesca* 8.2 (1984): 3-10.

Dunn, Peter N. *Spanish Picaresque Fiction. A New Literary History.* Ithaca: Cornell University Press, 1993.
Elias, Norbert. *Power and Civility.* Volume 2 of *The Civilizing Process.* Transl. by Edmund Jephcott. New York: Pantheon Books, 1982.
Elliott, John H. *The Count-Duke of Olivares. The Statesman in an Age of Decline.* New Haven: Yale University Press, 1986.
Estebanillo González. Eds. Nicholas Spadaccini y Anthony Zahareas. Madrid: Castalia, 1978. 2 vols.
Fernández de Navarrete, Pedro. *Conservación de Monarquías y discursos políticos sobre la gran consulta que el consejo...* (1619). Ed. de *BAE.* vol. 25. Madrid: Rivadeneyra, 1861. 449-546.
Forcione, Alban K. "At the Threshold of Modernity: Gracián's *El Criticón.*" *Rhetoric and Politics. Baltasar Gracián and the New World Order.* Eds. Nicholas Spadaccini and Jenaro Talens. Minneapolis: University of Minnesota Press, 1997. 3-70.

———. "La disociación cósmica de Gracián." *Nueva Revista de Filología Hispánica* 40 (1992): 419-450.
Friedman, Edward. "Ideologies of Discourse in Góngora's *Polifemo.*" *Cultural Authority in Golden Age Spain.* Eds. Marina S. Brownlee and Hans Ulrich Gumbrecht. Baltimore: The Johns Hopkins University Press, 1995. 51-78.

———. *The Antiheroine's Voice. Narrative Discourse and Transformations of the Picaresque.* Columbia: University of Missouri Press, 1987.
Gambin, Felice. "Saber y supervivencia. Anotaciones sobre el concepto de persona en Baltasar Gracián." *Actas del VI Seminario de Historia de la Filosofía Española e Iberoamericana.* Salamanca: Universidad de Salamanca, 1990. 369-380.
García, Carlos. *La desordenada codicia de los bienes ajenos.* Ed. Giulio Massano. Madrid: José Porrúa Turanzas, 1977.
Godzich, Wlad and Spadaccini, Nicholas. "Popular Culture and Spanish Literary History." *Literature among Discourses. The Spanish Golden Age.* Eds. Wlad Godzich and Nicholas Spadaccini. Minneapolis: University of Minnesota Press, 1986. 41-61.
Gómez Camacho, Francisco. "Introducción" to his edition of Luis de Molina's *Tratado sobre los cambios.* Madrid: Instituto de Estudios Fiscales, Instituto de Cooperación Iberoamericana, 1990.

———. "Introducción" to his edition of Luis de Molina's *Tratado sobre los préstamos y la usura.* Madrid: Instituto de Estudios Fiscales, Instituto de Cooperación Iberoamericana, 1989.
Gómez-Moriana, Antonio. *Discourse Analysis as Sociocriticism: The Spanish Golden Age.* Minneapolis: University of Minnesota Press, 1993.
González de Cellorigo, Martín. *Memorial de la política necesaria y útil restauración a la república de España* (1600). Ed. José L. Pérez de Ayala. Madrid: Instituto de Estudios Fiscales, Instituto de Cooperación Iberoamericana, 1991.
González-Echeverría, Roberto. *Celestina's Brood. Continuities of the Baroque in Spanish and Latin-American Literature.* Durham: Duke University Press, 1993.
Goux, Jean-Joseph. *The Coiners of Language.* Transl. by Jennifer Curtiss Gage. Norman: University of Oklahoma Press, 1994.
Gracián, Baltasar. *El héroe. El discreto. Oráculo manual y arte de prudencia.* Ed. Luys Santa Marina. Barcelona: Planeta, 1990.

———. *El Criticón.* Ed. Evaristo Correa Calderón. Madrid: Espasa-Calpe, 1971. 3 vols.

———. *Agudeza y arte de ingenio.* Ed. Evaristo Correa Calderón. Madrid: Castalia, 1969. 2 vols.
Grice-Hutchinson, Marjorie. *Economic Thought in Spain.* Eds. Laurence S. Moss and Christopher K. Ryan. Vermont: Elgar, 1993.

Habermas, Jürgen. *The Structural Transformation of the Public Sphere. An Inquiry into a Category of Bourgeois Society*. Transl. by Thomas Burger. Cambridge: The MIT Press, 1991.
Hamilton, Earl J. *American Treasure and the Price Revolution in Spain. 1501-1650*. New York: Octagon Books, 1970.
Hernández, M. Teresa. "La teoría literaria del conceptismo en Baltasar Gracián." *Estudios de Lingüística de la Universidad de Alicante* 3 (1985-1986): 7-46.
Hobbes, Thomas. *Leviathan*. Ed. Richard Tuck. Cambridge: Cambridge University Press, 1996.
Hoogstraten, Rudolf van. *Estructura mítica de la picaresca*. Madrid: Fundamentos, 1986.
Ife, B.W. *Reading and Fiction in Golden-Age Spain. A Platonist Critique and some Picaresque Replies*. Cambridge: Cambridge University Press, 1985.
Jones, Joseph R. "Hieroglyphics in *La Pícara Justina*." *Estudios literarios de hispanistas norteamericanos dedicados a Helmut Hatzfeld con motivo de su 80 aniversario*. Eds. Solá-Sole, Crisafulli, Damiani. Barcelona: Hispam, 1974. 415-429.
Kagan, Richard L. *Students and Society in Early Modern Spain*. Berkeley: University of California Press, 1974.
Kassier, Theodore L. *The Truth Disguised. Allegorical Structure and Technique in Gracián's* Criticón. London: Tamesis, 1976.
Langholm, Odd. *The Legacy of Scholasticism in Economic Thought. Antecedents of Choice and Power*. Cambridge: Cambridge University Press, 1998.
———. *Wealth and Money in the Aristotelian Tradition. A Study in Scholastic Economic Sources*. Oslo: Universitetsforlaget, 1983.
Lazarillo de Tormes. Ed. Joseph V. Ricapito. Madrid: Cátedra, 1983.
Lewis, Tom and Sánchez, Francisco J. "Introduction." *Culture and the State in Spain: 1550-1850*. Eds. Tom Lewis and Francisco J. Sánchez. New York: Garland Press, 1999. IX-XXIII.
Liñán y Verdugo, Antonio. *Guía y aviso de forasteros que vienen a esta corte*. Ed. Edisons Simons. Madrid: Editora Nacional, 1980.
López Bravo, Mateo. *Del rey y la raçón de governar* (1616-1627). In Henry Mechoulan, *Mateo López Bravo. Un socialista español del siglo XVII*. Madrid: Editora Nacional, 1977. 97-343.
López de Úbeda, Francisco. *La Pícara Justina*. Ed. A. Rey Hazas. Madrid: Editora Nacional, 1977.
Luna, Juan de. *Segunda Parte de la vida de Lazarillo de Tormes*. Ed. Pedro M. Piñero. Madrid: Cátedra, 1988.
Machiavelli, Niccolò. *The Prince*. Transl. by George Bull. New York: Penguin Books, 1999.
Maiorino, Giancarlo. "Picaresque Econopoetics: At the Watershed of Living Standards." *The Picaresque. Tradition and Displacement*. Ed. Giancarlo Maiorino. Minneapolis: University of Minnesota Press, 1996. 1-39.
Maravall, José Antonio. *La literatura picaresca desde la historia social*. Madrid: Taurus, 1986.
———. "From the Renaissance to the Baroque. The Diphasic Schema of a Social Crisis." *Literature among Discourses. The Spanish Golden Age*. Eds. Wlad Godzich and Nicholas Spadaccini. Minneapolis: The University of Minnesota Press, 1986. 3-40.
———. *Estado moderno y mentalidad social. Siglos XV a XVII*. Madrid: segunda edición, Alianza Editorial, 1986. 2 vols.
———. "Antropología y política en el pensamiento de Gracián." *Estudios de historia del pensamiento español. El siglo del Barroco*. Madrid: Cultura Hispánica, 1984. 333-373.

Maravall, José Antonio. *La cultura del Barroco. Análisis de una estructura histórica.* Barcelona: Ariel, 1980.

———. *Teatro y literatura en la sociedad barroca en el siglo diecisiete.* Madrid: Seminario y Ediciones, 1972.

———. *La oposición política bajo los Austrias.* Barcelona: Ariel, 1972.

———. *Las comunidades de Castilla, una primera revolución moderna.* Madrid: Revista de Occidente, 1970.

———. *El mundo social de La Celestina.* Madrid: Gredos, 1964.

Maritain, Jacques. *The Person and the Common Good.* New York: Charles Scribner's Sons, 1947.

Martin, Alfred von. *Sociology of the Renaissance.* Transl. by W.L. Luetkens. New York: Harper & Row, 1963.

Martz, Linda. *Poverty and Welfare in Habsburg Spain. The Example of Toledo.* Cambridge: Cambridge University Press, 1983.

Marx, Karl. *Capital* I. Translation by Ben Fowkes. New York: Penguin Classics, 1990.

Mercado, Tomás de. *Suma de tratos y contratos* (1569-1571). Ed. Nicolás Sánchez-Albornoz. Madrid: Instituto de Estudios Fiscales, 1977. 2 vols.

Molina, Luis de. *Tratado sobre los cambios* (1597). Ed. Francisco Gómez Camacho. Madrid: Instituto de Estudios Fiscales, Instituto de Cooperación Iberoamericana, 1990.

———. *Tratado sobre los préstamos y la usura* (1597). Ed. Francisco Gómez Camacho. Madrid: Instituto de Estudios Fiscales, Instituto de Cooperación Iberoamericana, 1989.

Moncada, Sancho de. *Restauración política de España* (1619). Ed. Jean Vilar. Madrid: Instituto de Estudios Fiscales, 1974.

Montalvo, Manuel. "La crisis del siglo XVII desde la atalaya de Mateo Alemán." *Revista de Occidente* 112 (Septiembre 1990): 116-135.

Norris Clark, N. *Person and Being.* Milwaukee: Markette University Press, 1993.

Olivares, Conde-Duque de. *Memoriales y cartas del Conde-Duque de Olivares.* Eds. John H. Elliott y José F. de la Peña. Madrid: Alfaguara, 1978.

Ortiz, Luis. *Memorial del contador Luis de Ortiz a Felipe II* (1558). Ed. Manuel Fernández Álvarez. *Anales de Economía* XVII (1957).

Pagden, Anthony. *Lords of All the World. Ideologies of Empire in Spain, Britain and France c.1500-c.1800.* New Haven: Yale University Press, 1995.

Parker, Alexander A. *Polyphemus and Galatea: A Study in the Interpretation of a Baroque Poem.* Austin: University of Texas Press, 1977.

Pérez Moreda, Vicente. "The Plague in Castile at the end of the Sixteenth Century and its Consequences."*The Castilian Crisis of the Seventeenth Century. New Perspectives on the Economic and Social History of Seventeenth-Century Spain.* Eds. I.A.A. Thompson and Bartolomé Yun Casalilla. Cambridge: Cambridge University Press, 1994. 32-59.

Perry, Mary Elizabeth. "The Politics of Race, Ethnicity, and Gender in the Making of the Spanish State." *Culture and the State in Spain: 1550-1850.* Eds. Tom Lewis and Francisco J. Sánchez. New York: Garland, 1999. 34-54.

Read, Malcolm K. "Cristóbal de Villalón: Language, Education, and the Absolutist State." *Culture and the State in Spain: 1550-1850.* Eds. Tom Lewis and Francisco J. Sánchez. New York: Garland, 1999. 1-33.

———. "Saving Appearances: Language and Commodification in Baltasar Gracián." *Rhetoric and Politics. Baltasar Gracián and the New World Order.* Eds. Nicholas Spadaccini and Jenaro Talens. Minneapolis: The University of Minnesota Press, 1997. 91-124.

———. *The Birth and Death of Language. Spanish Literature and Linguistics: 1300-1700.* Madrid: José Porrúa Turanzas, 1983.

Resina, Joan Ramon. "Cervantes's Confidence Games and the Refashioning of Totality." *MLN* 3.2 (1996): 218-253.
———. "El precio de una esposa." *Los usos del clásico*. Barcelona: Anthropos, 1991. 245-290.
Rey Hazas, Antonio. "La compleja faz de una pícara: Hacia una interpretación de *La Pícara Justina*." *Revista de Literatura* 45 nº 90, 1983. 87-109.
Rico, Francisco. *La novela picaresca y el punto de vista*. Barcelona: Seix Barral, 2000.
Rodríguez, Juan Carlos. *La literatura del pobre*. Granada: Comares, 1994.
Rodríguez-Matos, Carlos Antonio. *El narrador pícaro: Guzmán de Alfarache*. Madison: The Hispanic Seminar of Medieval Studies, 1985.
Rodríguez Puértolas, Julio. "*La Celestina* o la negación de la negación." *Literatura, Historia, Alienación*. Barcelona: Labor, 1976. 147-171.
Rojas, Fernando. *La Celestina*. Ed. Dorothy S. Severin. Madrid: Cátedra, 1995.
Ruiz Martín, Felipe. *Pequeño capitalismo. Gran capitalismo. Simón Ruiz y sus negocios en Florencia*. Barcelona: Crítica, 1990.
Salas Barbadillo, Jerónimo de. *La hija de Celestina y la Ingeniosa Elena*. Ed. J. Fradejas. Madrid: Instituto de Estudios Madrileños, 1983.
Salomon, Noël. *La vida rural castellana en tiempos de Felipe II*. Translation by Francesc Espinet. Barcelona: Ariel, 1982.
Sánchez, Francisco J. *Lectura y representación. Análisis cultural de las 'Novelas ejemplares.'* New York: Peter Lang, 1993.
Schumpeter, Joseph A. *History of Economic Analysis*. New York: Oxford University Press, 1954.
Shell, Marc. *Money, Language and Thought. Literary and Philosophical Economies from the Medieval to the Modern Era*. Berkeley: University of California Press, 1982.
Spadaccini, N. and Zahareas, A. "Introducción crítica" to *Estebanillo González*. Madrid: Castalia, 1978. Vol. 1, 9-120.
Suárez, Francisco. *A Treatise on Laws and God the Lawgiver*. Translation from Latin by G.L. Williams, A. Brown and J. Waldren. In *Selection from Three Works*. Oxford: Clarendon, 1944.
Vassberg, David E. *Land and Society in Golden Age Castile*. Cambridge: Cambridge University Press, 1984.
———. *La venta de tierras baldías, el comunitarismo agrario y la corona de Castilla durante el siglo XVI*. Madrid: Servicio de Publicaciones Agrarias, 1983.
Vázquez de Menchaca, Fernando. *Controversias fundamentales* (1564). Valladolid: Universidad de Valladolid, 1931.
Vega, José de la. *Confusión de confusiones. Diálogos curiosos entre un filósofo agudo, un mercader discreto y un accionista erudito...* (1688). Ed. facsimile. Madrid: Sociedad Española de Publicaciones, 1958.
Vilar, Pierre. *A History of Gold and Money. 1450-1920*. Translation by Judith White. London: New Left Books, 1976.
———. "Los primitivos españoles del pensamiento económico. 'Cuantitativismo' y 'bullonismo.'" *Crecimiento y desarrollo*. Barcelona: Ariel, 1976. 135-162.
———. "El problema de la formación del capitalismo."*Ibid*. 106-134.
———. "El tiempo del 'Quijote.'" *Ibid*. 332-346.
Vitoria, Francisco. *Obras*. Madrid: Biblioteca de Autores Cristianos, 1960.
Vives, Juan Luis. *Del socorro de los pobres, o de las necesidades humanas* (1526). Ed. *Biblioteca de Autores Españoles* vol. 65. Madrid: Rivadeneyra, 1873. 261-291.
Wallerstein, Immanuel. "The Bourgeois(ie) as Concept and Reality." In Etienne Balibar & Immanuel Wallerstein. *Race, Nation, Class. Ambiguous Identities*. London and New York: Verso, 1991. 135-152.

Wallerstein, Immanuel. *The Modern World System*. New York: Academic Press, 1974, 1980. 2 vols.
Williams, Raymond. *Keywords. A Vocabulary of Culture and Society*. New York: Oxford University Press, 1983.
Yndurain, Domingo. *Humanismo y Renacimiento en España*. Madrid: Cátedra, 1994.
Yun Casalilla, Bartolomé. *Sobre la transición al capitalismo en Castilla*. Salamanca: Junta de Castilla y León, 1987.
Zayas, María. *Tres novelas amorosas y tres desengaños amorosos*. Ed. A Redondo. Madrid: Castalia, 1989.

NORTH CAROLINA STUDIES IN THE ROMANCE LANGUAGES AND LITERATURES

I.S.B.N. Prefix 0-8078-

Recent Titles

THE RAVISHMENT OF PERSEPHONE: EPISTOLARY LYRIC IN THE *SIÈCLE DES LUMIÈRES*, by Julia K. De Pree. 1998. (No. 258). *-9262-9.*
CONVERTING FICTION: COUNTER REFORMATIONAL CLOSURE IN THE SECULAR LITERATURE OF GOLDEN AGE SPAIN, by David H. Darst. 1998. (No. 259). *-9263-7.*
GALDÓS'S *SEGUNDA MANERA*: RHETORICAL STRATEGIES AND AFFECTIVE RESPONSE, by Linda M. Willem. 1998. (No. 260). *-9264-5.*
A MEDIEVAL PILGRIM'S COMPANION. REASSESSING *EL LIBRO DE LOS HUÉSPEDES* (ESCORIAL MS. h.I.13), by Thomas D. Spaccarelli. 1998. (No. 261). *-9265-3.*
'PUEBLOS ENFERMOS': THE DISCOURSE OF ILLNESS IN THE TURN-OF-THE-CENTURY SPANISH AND LATIN AMERICAN ESSAY, by Michael Aronna. 1999. (No. 262). *-9266-1.*
RESONANT THEMES. LITERATURE, HISTORY, AND THE ARTS IN NINETEENTH- AND TWENTIETH-CENTURY EUROPE. ESSAYS IN HONOR OF VICTOR BROMBERT, by Stirling Haig. 1999. (No. 263). *-9267-X.*
RAZA, GÉNERO E HIBRIDEZ EN *EL LAZARILLO DE CIEGOS CAMINANTES*, por Mariselle Meléndez. 1999. (No. 264). *-9268-8.*
DEL ESCENARIO A LA PANTALLA: LA ADAPTACIÓN CINEMATOGRÁFICA DEL TEATRO ESPAÑOL, por María Asunción Gómez. 2000. (No. 265). *-9269-6.*
THE LEPER IN BLUE: COERCIVE PERFORMANCE AND THE CONTEMPORARY LATIN AMERICAN THEATER, by Amalia Gladhart. 2000. (No. 266). *-9270-X.*
THE CHARM OF CATASTROPHE: A STUDY OF RABELAIS'S *QUART LIVRE*, by Alice Fiola Berry. 2000. (No. 267). *-9271-8.*
PUERTO RICAN CULTURAL IDENTITY AND THE WORK OF LUIS RAFAEL SÁNCHEZ, by John Dimitri Perivolaris. 2000. (No. 268). *-9272-6.*
MANNERISM AND BAROQUE IN SEVENTEENTH-CENTURY FRENCH POETRY: THE EXAMPLE OF TRISTAN L'HERMITE, by James Crenshaw Shepard. 2001. (No. 269). *-9273-4.*
RECLAIMING THE BODY: MARÍA DE ZAYA'S EARLY MODERN FEMINISM, by Lisa Vollendorf. 2001. (No. 270). *-9274-2.*
FORGED GENEALOGIES: SAINT-JOHN PERSE'S CONVERSATIONS WITH CULTURE, by Carol Rigolot. 2001. (No. 271). *-9275-0.*
VISIONES DE ESTEREOSCOPIO (PARADIGMA DE HIBRIDACIÓN EN EL ARTE Y LA NARRATIVA DE LA VANGUARDIA ESPAÑOLA), por María Soledad Fernández Utrera. 2001. (No. 272). *-9276-9.*
TRANSPOSING ART INTO TEXTS IN FRENCH ROMANTIC LITERATURE, by Henry F. Majewski. 2002. (No. 273). *-9277-7.*
IMAGES IN MIND: LOVESICKNESS, SPANISH SENTIMENTAL FICTION AND *DON QUIJOTE*, by Robert Folger. 2002. (No. 274). *-9278-5.*
INDISCERNIBLE COUNTERPARTS: THE INVENTION OF THE TEXT IN FRENCH CLASSICAL DRAMA, by Christopher Braider. 2002. (No. 275). *-9279-3.*
SAVAGE SIGHT/CONSTRUCTED NOISE. POETIC ADAPTATIONS OF PAINTERLY TECHNIQUES IN THE FRENCH AND AMERICAN AVANT-GARDES, by David LeHardy Sweet. 2003. (No. 276). *-9281-5.*
AN EARLY BOURGEOIS LITERATURE IN GOLDEN AGE SPAIN. *LAZARILLO DE TORMES, GUZMÁN DE ALFARACHE* AND BALTASAR GRACIÁN, by Francisco J. Sánchez. 2003. (No. 277). *-9280-7.*

When ordering please cite the *ISBN Prefix* plus the last four digits for each title.

Send orders to: University of North Carolina Press
P.O. Box 2288
Chapel Hill, NC 27515-2288
U.S.A.
www.uncpress.unc.edu
FAX: 919 966-3829

www.ingramcontent.com/pod-product-compliance
Lightning Source LLC
Chambersburg PA
CBHW020741230426
43665CB00009B/514